Consumer Rights Act 2015

CHAPTER 15

Explanatory Notes are available separately

AF719462

GRAN*GIS* UK Publishing

Adapted and published by GRANGIS (Grand Register Library).
Online: www.grangis.com
E-mail: contact@grangis.com

In this version:
ISBN: 979-8-88559-013-6

Note: This is the original version (as it was originally enacted). Title, sub-title and the generated date is as marked on the pages.

Consumer Rights Act 2015

CHAPTER 15

CONSUMER RIGHTS ACT 2015

PART 1

CONSUMER CONTRACTS FOR GOODS, DIGITAL CONTENT AND SERVICES

CHAPTER 1

INTRODUCTION

CHAPTER 2

GOODS

What goods contracts are covered?

What statutory rights are there under a goods contract?

31 Omit section 79 (general powers of inspection and entry).
32 Before section 80 insert— Investigatory powers For the investigatory powers available to a local weights and...
33 In section 80 omit "or the packaged goods regulations".
34 In section 81(1)(b) (failure to provide assistance or information) omit...
35 (1) Section 84 (penalties) is amended as follows.
36 In paragraph 21(2)(b) of Schedule 11 (application of provisions applying...
37 Consumer Protection Act 1987 (c. 43)
38 In section 27 (enforcement) after subsection (3) insert—
39 Omit section 28 (test purchases).
40 (1) Section 29 (powers of search etc) is amended as...
41 (1) Section 30 (provisions supplemental to section 29) is amended...
42 In section 31(1) (power of customs officer to detain goods)...
43 In section 32(1) (obstruction of authorised officer)—
44 In section 33(1) (appeals against detention of goods) for "any...
45 In section 34(1) (compensation for seizure and detention) for "29"...
46 In section 44(4) (service of documents)— (a) omit "28(2) or",...
47 Education Reform Act 1988 (c. 40)
48 Copyright, Designs and Patents Act 1988 (c. 48)
49 (1) Section 107A (enforcement of section 107 by local weights...
50 (1) Section 198A (enforcement of section 198 by local weights...
51 Clean Air Act 1993 (c. 11)
52 (1) Section 30 (regulations about motor fuel) is amended as...
53 In section 31 (regulations about sulphur content of oil fuel...
54 In section 32(4) (powers of entry not to apply in...
55 In section 49(1) (unjustified disclosures of information) after "this Act"...
56 In section 56 (rights of entry and inspection etc) after...
57 In section 58(1) (power of local authorities to obtain information)—...
58 Sunday Trading Act 1994 (c. 20)
59 Trade Marks Act 1994 (c. 26)
60 Olympic Symbol etc (Protection) Act 1995 (c. 32)
61 Criminal Justice and Police Act 2001 (c. 16)
62 In section 57(1) (retention of seized items)—
63 (1) Section 65 (meaning of legal privilege) is amended as...
64 In section 66(4) (construction of references to a search)—
65 (1) Part 1 of Schedule 1 (powers to which section...
66 (1) Part 1 of Schedule 2 (application of enactments) is...
67 Enterprise Act 2002 (c. 40)
68 Omit section 224 (power of CMA to require the provision...
69 Omit section 225 (power of other enforcer to require the...
70 Omit section 226 (procedure for notices requiring information).
71 Omit section 227 (enforcement of notices).
72 Omit section 227A (power to enter premises without warrant).
73 Omit section 227B (powers exercisable on the premises).
74 Omit section 227C (power to enter premises with warrant).
75 Omit section 227D (ancillary provisions about powers of entry).
76 Omit section 227E (obstructing, or failing to co-operate with, powers...
77 Omit section 227F (retention of documents and goods).
78 Before section 228 (but after the italic heading "Miscellaneous") insert —...
79 In section 228 (evidence) omit subsection (4).

Consumer Rights Act 2015

2015 CHAPTER 15

An Act to amend the law relating to the rights of consumers and protection of their interests; to make provision about investigatory powers for enforcing the regulation of traders; to make provision about private actions in competition law and the Competition Appeal Tribunal; and for connected purposes. [26th March 2015]

BE IT ENACTED by the Queen's most Excellent Majesty, by and with the advice and consent of the Lords Spiritual and Temporal, and Commons, in this present Parliament assembled, and by the authority of the same, as follows:—

PART 1

CONSUMER CONTRACTS FOR GOODS, DIGITAL CONTENT AND SERVICES

CHAPTER 1

INTRODUCTION

1 Where Part 1 applies

(1) This Part applies where there is an agreement between a trader and a consumer for the trader to supply goods, digital content or services, if the agreement is a contract.

(2) It applies whether the contract is written or oral or implied from the parties' conduct, or more than one of these combined.

(3) Any of Chapters 2, 3 and 4 may apply to a contract—

- (a) if it is a contract for the trader to supply goods, see Chapter 2;
- (b) if it is a contract for the trader to supply digital content, see Chapter 3 (also, subsection (6));

(c) if it is a contract for the trader to supply a service, see Chapter 4 (also, subsection (6)).

(4) In each case the Chapter applies even if the contract also covers something covered by another Chapter (a mixed contract).

(5) Two or all three of those Chapters may apply to a mixed contract.

(6) For provisions about particular mixed contracts, see—
(a) section 15 (goods and installation);
(b) section 16 (goods and digital content).

(7) For other provision applying to contracts to which this Part applies, see Part 2 (unfair terms).

2 Key definitions

(1) These definitions apply in this Part (as well as the definitions in section 59).

(2) "Trader" means a person acting for purposes relating to that person's trade, business, craft or profession, whether acting personally or through another person acting in the trader's name or on the trader's behalf.

(3) "Consumer" means an individual acting for purposes that are wholly or mainly outside that individual's trade, business, craft or profession.

(4) A trader claiming that an individual was not acting for purposes wholly or mainly outside the individual's trade, business, craft or profession must prove it.

(5) For the purposes of Chapter 2, except to the extent mentioned in subsection (6), a person is not a consumer in relation to a sales contract if—
(a) the goods are second hand goods sold at public auction, and
(b) individuals have the opportunity of attending the sale in person.

(6) A person is a consumer in relation to such a contract for the purposes of—
(a) sections 11(4) and (5), 12, 28 and 29, and
(b) the other provisions of Chapter 2 as they apply in relation to those sections.

(7) "Business" includes the activities of any government department or local or public authority.

(8) "Goods" means any tangible moveable items, but that includes water, gas and electricity if and only if they are put up for supply in a limited volume or set quantity.

(9) "Digital content" means data which are produced and supplied in digital form.

CHAPTER 2

GOODS

What goods contracts are covered?

3 Contracts covered by this Chapter

(1) This Chapter applies to a contract for a trader to supply goods to a consumer.

(2) It applies only if the contract is one of these (defined for the purposes of this Part in sections 5 to 8)—
- (a) a sales contract;
- (b) a contract for the hire of goods;
- (c) a hire-purchase agreement;
- (d) a contract for transfer of goods.

(3) It does not apply—
- (a) to a contract for a trader to supply coins or notes to a consumer for use as currency;
- (b) to a contract for goods to be sold by way of execution or otherwise by authority of law;
- (c) to a contract intended to operate as a mortgage, pledge, charge or other security;
- (d) in relation to England and Wales or Northern Ireland, to a contract made by deed and for which the only consideration is the presumed consideration imported by the deed;
- (e) in relation to Scotland, to a gratuitous contract.

(4) A contract to which this Chapter applies is referred to in this Part as a "contract to supply goods".

(5) Contracts to supply goods include—
- (a) contracts entered into between one part owner and another;
- (b) contracts for the transfer of an undivided share in goods;
- (c) contracts that are absolute and contracts that are conditional.

(6) Subsection (1) is subject to any provision of this Chapter that applies a section or part of a section to only some of the kinds of contracts listed in subsection (2).

(7) A mixed contract (see section 1(4)) may be a contract of any of those kinds.

4 Ownership of goods

(1) In this Chapter ownership of goods means the general property in goods, not merely a special property.

(2) For the time when ownership of goods is transferred, see in particular the following provisions of the Sale of Goods Act 1979 (which relate to contracts of sale)—

section 16:	goods must be ascertained

section 17:	property passes when intended to pass
section 18:	rules for ascertaining intention
section 19:	reservation of right of disposal
section 20A:	undivided shares in goods forming part of a bulk
section 20B:	deemed consent by co-owner to dealings in bulk goods

5 Sales contracts

(1) A contract is a sales contract if under it—

(a) the trader transfers or agrees to transfer ownership of goods to the consumer, and

(b) the consumer pays or agrees to pay the price.

(2) A contract is a sales contract (whether or not it would be one under subsection (1)) if under the contract—

(a) goods are to be manufactured or produced and the trader agrees to supply them to the consumer,

(b) on being supplied, the goods will be owned by the consumer, and

(c) the consumer pays or agrees to pay the price.

(3) A sales contract may be conditional (see section 3(5)), but in this Part "conditional sales contract" means a sales contract under which—

(a) the price for the goods or part of it is payable by instalments, and

(b) the trader retains ownership of the goods until the conditions specified in the contract (for the payment of instalments or otherwise) are met;

and it makes no difference whether or not the consumer possesses the goods.

6 Contracts for the hire of goods

(1) A contract is for the hire of goods if under it the trader gives or agrees to give the consumer possession of the goods with the right to use them, subject to the terms of the contract, for a period determined in accordance with the contract.

(2) But a contract is not for the hire of goods if it is a hire-purchase agreement.

7 Hire-purchase agreements

(1) A contract is a hire-purchase agreement if it meets the two conditions set out below.

(2) The first condition is that under the contract goods are hired by the trader in return for periodical payments by the consumer (and "hired" is to be read in accordance with section 6(1)).

(3) The second condition is that under the contract ownership of the goods will transfer to the consumer if the terms of the contract are complied with and—

(a) the consumer exercises an option to buy the goods,

(b) any party to the contract does an act specified in it, or

(c) an event specified in the contract occurs.

(4) But a contract is not a hire-purchase agreement if it is a conditional sales contract.

8 Contracts for transfer of goods

A contract to supply goods is a contract for transfer of goods if under it the trader transfers or agrees to transfer ownership of the goods to the consumer and—

(a) the consumer provides or agrees to provide consideration otherwise than by paying a price, or

(b) the contract is, for any other reason, not a sales contract or a hire-purchase agreement.

What statutory rights are there under a goods contract?

9 Goods to be of satisfactory quality

(1) Every contract to supply goods is to be treated as including a term that the quality of the goods is satisfactory.

(2) The quality of goods is satisfactory if they meet the standard that a reasonable person would consider satisfactory, taking account of—

(a) any description of the goods,

(b) the price or other consideration for the goods (if relevant), and

(c) all the other relevant circumstances (see subsection (5)).

(3) The quality of goods includes their state and condition; and the following aspects (among others) are in appropriate cases aspects of the quality of goods—

(a) fitness for all the purposes for which goods of that kind are usually supplied;

(b) appearance and finish;

(c) freedom from minor defects;

(d) safety;

(e) durability.

(4) The term mentioned in subsection (1) does not cover anything which makes the quality of the goods unsatisfactory—

(a) which is specifically drawn to the consumer's attention before the contract is made,

(b) where the consumer examines the goods before the contract is made, which that examination ought to reveal, or

(c) in the case of a contract to supply goods by sample, which would have been apparent on a reasonable examination of the sample.

(5) The relevant circumstances mentioned in subsection (2)(c) include any public statement about the specific characteristics of the goods made by the trader, the producer or any representative of the trader or the producer.

(6) That includes, in particular, any public statement made in advertising or labelling.

(7) But a public statement is not a relevant circumstance for the purposes of subsection (2)(c) if the trader shows that—

(a) when the contract was made, the trader was not, and could not reasonably have been, aware of the statement,

(b) before the contract was made, the statement had been publicly withdrawn or, to the extent that it contained anything which was incorrect or misleading, it had been publicly corrected, or

(c) the consumer's decision to contract for the goods could not have been influenced by the statement.

(8) In a contract to supply goods a term about the quality of the goods may be treated as included as a matter of custom.

(9) See section 19 for a consumer's rights if the trader is in breach of a term that this section requires to be treated as included in a contract.

10 Goods to be fit for particular purpose

(1) Subsection (3) applies to a contract to supply goods if before the contract is made the consumer makes known to the trader (expressly or by implication) any particular purpose for which the consumer is contracting for the goods.

(2) Subsection (3) also applies to a contract to supply goods if—

(a) the goods were previously sold by a credit-broker to the trader,

(b) in the case of a sales contract or contract for transfer of goods, the consideration or part of it is a sum payable by instalments, and

(c) before the contract is made, the consumer makes known to the credit-broker (expressly or by implication) any particular purpose for which the consumer is contracting for the goods.

(3) The contract is to be treated as including a term that the goods are reasonably fit for that purpose, whether or not that is a purpose for which goods of that kind are usually supplied.

(4) Subsection (3) does not apply if the circumstances show that the consumer does not rely, or it is unreasonable for the consumer to rely, on the skill or judgment of the trader or credit-broker.

(5) In a contract to supply goods a term about the fitness of the goods for a particular purpose may be treated as included as a matter of custom.

(6) See section 19 for a consumer's rights if the trader is in breach of a term that this section requires to be treated as included in a contract.

11 Goods to be as described

(1) Every contract to supply goods by description is to be treated as including a term that the goods will match the description.

(2) If the supply is by sample as well as by description, it is not sufficient that the bulk of the goods matches the sample if the goods do not also match the description.

(3) A supply of goods is not prevented from being a supply by description just because—

(a) the goods are exposed for supply, and

(b) they are selected by the consumer.

(4) Any information that is provided by the trader about the goods and is information mentioned in paragraph (a) of Schedule 1 or 2 to the Consumer Contracts (Information, Cancellation and Additional Charges) Regulations 2013 (SI 2013/3134) (main characteristics of goods) is to be treated as included as a term of the contract.

(5) A change to any of that information, made before entering into the contract or later, is not effective unless expressly agreed between the consumer and the trader.

(6) See section 2(5) and (6) for the application of subsections (4) and (5) where goods are sold at public auction.

(7) See section 19 for a consumer's rights if the trader is in breach of a term that this section requires to be treated as included in a contract.

12 Other pre-contract information included in contract

(1) This section applies to any contract to supply goods.

(2) Where regulation 9, 10 or 13 of the Consumer Contracts (Information, Cancellation and Additional Charges) Regulations 2013 (SI 2013/3134) required the trader to provide information to the consumer before the contract became binding, any of that information that was provided by the trader other than information about the goods and mentioned in paragraph (a) of Schedule 1 or 2 to the Regulations (main characteristics of goods) is to be treated as included as a term of the contract.

(3) A change to any of that information, made before entering into the contract or later, is not effective unless expressly agreed between the consumer and the trader.

(4) See section 2(5) and (6) for the application of this section where goods are sold at public auction.

(5) See section 19 for a consumer's rights if the trader is in breach of a term that this section requires to be treated as included in the contract.

13 Goods to match a sample

(1) This section applies to a contract to supply goods by reference to a sample of the goods that is seen or examined by the consumer before the contract is made.

(2) Every contract to which this section applies is to be treated as including a term that—
   (a) the goods will match the sample except to the extent that any differences between the sample and the goods are brought to the consumer's attention before the contract is made, and
   (b) the goods will be free from any defect that makes their quality unsatisfactory and that would not be apparent on a reasonable examination of the sample.

(3) See section 19 for a consumer's rights if the trader is in breach of a term that this section requires to be treated as included in a contract.

14 Goods to match a model seen or examined

(1) This section applies to a contract to supply goods by reference to a model of the goods that is seen or examined by the consumer before entering into the contract.

(2) Every contract to which this section applies is to be treated as including a term that the goods will match the model except to the extent that any differences between the model and the goods are brought to the consumer's attention before the consumer enters into the contract.

(3) See section 19 for a consumer's rights if the trader is in breach of a term that this section requires to be treated as included in a contract.

15 Installation as part of conformity of the goods with the contract

(1) Goods do not conform to a contract to supply goods if—

(a) installation of the goods forms part of the contract,

(b) the goods are installed by the trader or under the trader's responsibility, and

(c) the goods are installed incorrectly.

(2) See section 19 for the effect of goods not conforming to the contract.

16 Goods not conforming to contract if digital content does not conform

(1) Goods (whether or not they conform otherwise to a contract to supply goods) do not conform to it if—

(a) the goods are an item that includes digital content, and

(b) the digital content does not conform to the contract to supply that content (for which see section 42(1)).

(2) See section 19 for the effect of goods not conforming to the contract.

17 Trader to have right to supply the goods etc

(1) Every contract to supply goods, except one within subsection (4), is to be treated as including a term—

(a) in the case of a contract for the hire of goods, that at the beginning of the period of hire the trader must have the right to transfer possession of the goods by way of hire for that period,

(b) in any other case, that the trader must have the right to sell or transfer the goods at the time when ownership of the goods is to be transferred.

(2) Every contract to supply goods, except a contract for the hire of goods or a contract within subsection (4), is to be treated as including a term that—

(a) the goods are free from any charge or encumbrance not disclosed or known to the consumer before entering into the contract,

(b) the goods will remain free from any such charge or encumbrance until ownership of them is to be transferred, and

(c) the consumer will enjoy quiet possession of the goods except so far as it may be disturbed by the owner or other person entitled to the benefit of any charge or encumbrance so disclosed or known.

(3) Every contract for the hire of goods is to be treated as including a term that the consumer will enjoy quiet possession of the goods for the period of the hire except so far as the possession may be disturbed by the owner or other person entitled to the benefit of any charge or encumbrance disclosed or known to the consumer before entering into the contract.

(4) This subsection applies to a contract if the contract shows, or the circumstances when they enter into the contract imply, that the trader and the consumer intend the trader to transfer only—

(a) whatever title the trader has, even if it is limited, or
(b) whatever title a third person has, even if it is limited.

(5) Every contract within subsection (4) is to be treated as including a term that all charges or encumbrances known to the trader and not known to the consumer were disclosed to the consumer before entering into the contract.

(6) Every contract within subsection (4) is to be treated as including a term that the consumer's quiet possession of the goods—
(a) will not be disturbed by the trader, and
(b) will not be disturbed by a person claiming through or under the trader, unless that person is claiming under a charge or encumbrance that was disclosed or known to the consumer before entering into the contract.

(7) If subsection (4)(b) applies (transfer of title that a third person has), the contract is also to be treated as including a term that the consumer's quiet possession of the goods—
(a) will not be disturbed by the third person, and
(b) will not be disturbed by a person claiming through or under the third person, unless the claim is under a charge or encumbrance that was disclosed or known to the consumer before entering into the contract.

(8) In the case of a contract for the hire of goods, this section does not affect the right of the trader to repossess the goods where the contract provides or is to be treated as providing for this.

(9) See section 19 for a consumer's rights if the trader is in breach of a term that this section requires to be treated as included in a contract.

18 No other requirement to treat term about quality or fitness as included

(1) Except as provided by sections 9, 10, 13 and 16, a contract to supply goods is not to be treated as including any term about the quality of the goods or their fitness for any particular purpose, unless the term is expressly included in the contract.

(2) Subsection (1) is subject to provision made by any other enactment (whenever passed or made).

What remedies are there if statutory rights under a goods contract are not met?

19 Consumer's rights to enforce terms about goods

(1) In this section and sections 22 to 24 references to goods conforming to a contract are references to—
(a) the goods conforming to the terms described in sections 9, 10, 11, 13 and 14,
(b) the goods not failing to conform to the contract under section 15 or 16, and
(c) the goods conforming to requirements that are stated in the contract.

(2) But, for the purposes of this section and sections 22 to 24, a failure to conform as mentioned in subsection (1)(a) to (c) is not a failure to conform to the contract if it has its origin in materials supplied by the consumer.

(3) If the goods do not conform to the contract because of a breach of any of the terms described in sections 9, 10, 11, 13 and 14, or if they do not conform to the contract

under section 16, the consumer's rights (and the provisions about them and when they are available) are—

(a) the short-term right to reject (sections 20 and 22);

(b) the right to repair or replacement (section 23); and

(c) the right to a price reduction or the final right to reject (sections 20 and 24).

(4) If the goods do not conform to the contract under section 15 or because of a breach of requirements that are stated in the contract, the consumer's rights (and the provisions about them and when they are available) are—

(a) the right to repair or replacement (section 23); and

(b) the right to a price reduction or the final right to reject (sections 20 and 24).

(5) If the trader is in breach of a term that section 12 requires to be treated as included in the contract, the consumer has the right to recover from the trader the amount of any costs incurred by the consumer as a result of the breach, up to the amount of the price paid or the value of other consideration given for the goods.

(6) If the trader is in breach of the term that section 17(1) (right to supply etc) requires to be treated as included in the contract, the consumer has a right to reject (see section 20 for provisions about that right and when it is available).

(7) Subsections (3) to (6) are subject to section 25 and subsections (3)(a) and (6) are subject to section 26.

(8) Section 28 makes provision about remedies for breach of a term about the time for delivery of goods.

(9) This Chapter does not prevent the consumer seeking other remedies—

(a) for a breach of a term that this Chapter requires to be treated as included in the contract,

(b) on the grounds that, under section 15 or 16, goods do not conform to the contract, or

(c) for a breach of a requirement stated in the contract.

(10) Those other remedies may be ones—

(a) in addition to a remedy referred to in subsections (3) to (6) (but not so as to recover twice for the same loss), or

(b) instead of such a remedy, or

(c) where no such remedy is provided for.

(11) Those other remedies include any of the following that is open to the consumer in the circumstances—

(a) claiming damages;

(b) seeking specific performance;

(c) seeking an order for specific implement;

(d) relying on the breach against a claim by the trader for the price;

(e) for breach of an express term, exercising a right to treat the contract as at an end.

(12) It is not open to the consumer to treat the contract as at an end for breach of a term that this Chapter requires to be treated as included in the contract, or on the grounds that, under section 15 or 16, goods do not conform to the contract, except as provided by subsections (3), (4) and (6).

(13) In this Part, treating a contract as at an end means treating it as repudiated.

(14) For the purposes of subsections (3)(b) and (c) and (4), goods which do not conform to the contract at any time within the period of six months beginning with the day on which the goods were delivered to the consumer must be taken not to have conformed to it on that day.

(15) Subsection (14) does not apply if—
- (a) it is established that the goods did conform to the contract on that day, or
- (b) its application is incompatible with the nature of the goods or with how they fail to conform to the contract.

20 Right to reject

(1) The short-term right to reject is subject to section 22.

(2) The final right to reject is subject to section 24.

(3) The right to reject under section 19(6) is not limited by those sections.

(4) Each of these rights entitles the consumer to reject the goods and treat the contract as at an end, subject to subsections (20) and (21).

(5) The right is exercised if the consumer indicates to the trader that the consumer is rejecting the goods and treating the contract as at an end.

(6) The indication may be something the consumer says or does, but it must be clear enough to be understood by the trader.

(7) From the time when the right is exercised—
- (a) the trader has a duty to give the consumer a refund, subject to subsection (18), and
- (b) the consumer has a duty to make the goods available for collection by the trader or (if there is an agreement for the consumer to return rejected goods) to return them as agreed.

(8) Whether or not the consumer has a duty to return the rejected goods, the trader must bear any reasonable costs of returning them, other than any costs incurred by the consumer in returning the goods in person to the place where the consumer took physical possession of them.

(9) The consumer's entitlement to receive a refund works as follows.

(10) To the extent that the consumer paid money under the contract, the consumer is entitled to receive back the same amount of money.

(11) To the extent that the consumer transferred anything else under the contract, the consumer is entitled to receive back the same amount of what the consumer transferred, unless subsection (12) applies.

(12) To the extent that the consumer transferred under the contract something for which the same amount of the same thing cannot be substituted, the consumer is entitled to receive back in its original state whatever the consumer transferred.

(13) If the contract is for the hire of goods, the entitlement to a refund extends only to anything paid or otherwise transferred for a period of hire that the consumer does not get because the contract is treated as at an end.

(14) If the contract is a hire-purchase agreement or a conditional sales contract and the contract is treated as at an end before the whole of the price has been paid, the entitlement to a refund extends only to the part of the price paid.

(15) A refund under this section must be given without undue delay, and in any event within 14 days beginning with the day on which the trader agrees that the consumer is entitled to a refund.

(16) If the consumer paid money under the contract, the trader must give the refund using the same means of payment as the consumer used, unless the consumer expressly agrees otherwise.

(17) The trader must not impose any fee on the consumer in respect of the refund.

(18) There is no entitlement to receive a refund—

(a) if none of subsections (10) to (12) applies,

(b) to the extent that anything to which subsection (12) applies cannot be given back in its original state, or

(c) where subsection (13) applies, to the extent that anything the consumer transferred under the contract cannot be divided so as to give back only the amount, or part of the amount, to which the consumer is entitled.

(19) It may be open to a consumer to claim damages where there is no entitlement to receive a refund, or because of the limits of the entitlement, or instead of a refund.

(20) Subsection (21) qualifies the application in relation to England and Wales and Northern Ireland of the rights mentioned in subsections (1) to (3) where—

(a) the contract is a severable contract,

(b) in relation to the final right to reject, the contract is a contract for the hire of goods, a hire-purchase agreement or a contract for transfer of goods, and

(c) section 26(3) does not apply.

(21) The consumer is entitled, depending on the terms of the contract and the circumstances of the case—

(a) to reject the goods to which a severable obligation relates and treat that obligation as at an end (so that the entitlement to a refund relates only to what the consumer paid or transferred in relation to that obligation), or

(b) to exercise any of the rights mentioned in subsections (1) to (3) in respect of the whole contract.

21 Partial rejection of goods

(1) If the consumer has any of the rights mentioned in section 20(1) to (3), but does not reject all of the goods and treat the contract as at an end, the consumer—

(a) may reject some or all of the goods that do not conform to the contract, but

(b) may not reject any goods that do conform to the contract.

(2) If the consumer is entitled to reject the goods in an instalment, but does not reject all of those goods, the consumer—

(a) may reject some or all of the goods in the instalment that do not conform to the contract, but

(b) may not reject any goods in the instalment that do conform to the contract.

(3) If any of the goods form a commercial unit, the consumer cannot reject some of those goods without also rejecting the rest of them.

(4) A unit is a "commercial unit" if division of the unit would materially impair the value of the goods or the character of the unit.

(5) The consumer rejects goods under this section by indicating to the trader that the consumer is rejecting the goods.

(6) The indication may be something the consumer says or does, but it must be clear enough to be understood by the trader.

(7) From the time when a consumer rejects goods under this section—

(a) the trader has a duty to give the consumer a refund in respect of those goods (subject to subsection (10)), and

(b) the consumer has a duty to make those goods available for collection by the trader or (if there is an agreement for the consumer to return rejected goods) to return them as agreed.

(8) Whether or not the consumer has a duty to return the rejected goods, the trader must bear any reasonable costs of returning them, other than any costs incurred by the consumer in returning those goods in person to the place where the consumer took physical possession of them.

(9) Section 20(10) to (17) apply to a consumer's right to receive a refund under this section (and in section 20(13) and (14) references to the contract being treated as at an end are to be read as references to goods being rejected).

(10) That right does not apply—

(a) if none of section 20(10) to (12) applies,

(b) to the extent that anything to which section 20(12) applies cannot be given back in its original state, or

(c) to the extent that anything the consumer transferred under the contract cannot be divided so as to give back only the amount, or part of the amount, to which the consumer is entitled.

(11) It may be open to a consumer to claim damages where there is no right to receive a refund, or because of the limits of the right, or instead of a refund.

(12) References in this section to goods conforming to a contract are to be read in accordance with section 19(1) and (2), but they also include the goods conforming to the terms described in section 17.

(13) Where section 20(21)(a) applies the reference in subsection (1) to the consumer treating the contract as at an end is to be read as a reference to the consumer treating the severable obligation as at an end.

22 Time limit for short-term right to reject

(1) A consumer who has the short-term right to reject loses it if the time limit for exercising it passes without the consumer exercising it, unless the trader and the consumer agree that it may be exercised later.

(2) An agreement under which the short-term right to reject would be lost before the time limit passes is not binding on the consumer.

(3) The time limit for exercising the short-term right to reject (unless subsection (4) applies) is the end of 30 days beginning with the first day after these have all happened—

- (a) ownership or (in the case of a contract for the hire of goods, a hire-purchase agreement or a conditional sales contract) possession of the goods has been transferred to the consumer,
- (b) the goods have been delivered, and
- (c) where the contract requires the trader to install the goods or take other action to enable the consumer to use them, the trader has notified the consumer that the action has been taken.

(4) If any of the goods are of a kind that can reasonably be expected to perish after a shorter period, the time limit for exercising the short-term right to reject in relation to those goods is the end of that shorter period (but without affecting the time limit in relation to goods that are not of that kind).

(5) Subsections (3) and (4) do not prevent the consumer exercising the short-term right to reject before something mentioned in subsection (3)(a), (b) or (c) has happened.

(6) If the consumer requests or agrees to the repair or replacement of goods, the period mentioned in subsection (3) or (4) stops running for the length of the waiting period.

(7) If goods supplied by the trader in response to that request or agreement do not conform to the contract, the time limit for exercising the short-term right to reject is then either—

- (a) 7 days after the waiting period ends, or
- (b) if later, the original time limit for exercising that right, extended by the waiting period.

(8) The waiting period—

- (a) begins with the day the consumer requests or agrees to the repair or replacement of the goods, and
- (b) ends with the day on which the consumer receives goods supplied by the trader in response to the request or agreement.

23 Right to repair or replacement

(1) This section applies if the consumer has the right to repair or replacement (see section 19(3) and (4)).

(2) If the consumer requires the trader to repair or replace the goods, the trader must—

- (a) do so within a reasonable time and without significant inconvenience to the consumer, and
- (b) bear any necessary costs incurred in doing so (including in particular the cost of any labour, materials or postage).

(3) The consumer cannot require the trader to repair or replace the goods if that remedy (the repair or the replacement)—

(a) is impossible, or

(b) is disproportionate compared to the other of those remedies.

(4) Either of those remedies is disproportionate compared to the other if it imposes costs on the trader which, compared to those imposed by the other, are unreasonable, taking into account—

(a) the value which the goods would have if they conformed to the contract,

(b) the significance of the lack of conformity, and

(c) whether the other remedy could be effected without significant inconvenience to the consumer.

(5) Any question as to what is a reasonable time or significant inconvenience is to be determined taking account of—

(a) the nature of the goods, and

(b) the purpose for which the goods were acquired.

(6) A consumer who requires or agrees to the repair of goods cannot require the trader to replace them, or exercise the short-term right to reject, without giving the trader a reasonable time to repair them (unless giving the trader that time would cause significant inconvenience to the consumer).

(7) A consumer who requires or agrees to the replacement of goods cannot require the trader to repair them, or exercise the short-term right to reject, without giving the trader a reasonable time to replace them (unless giving the trader that time would cause significant inconvenience to the consumer).

(8) In this Chapter, "repair" in relation to goods that do not conform to a contract, means making them conform.

24 Right to price reduction or final right to reject

(1) The right to a price reduction is the right—

(a) to require the trader to reduce by an appropriate amount the price the consumer is required to pay under the contract, or anything else the consumer is required to transfer under the contract, and

(b) to receive a refund from the trader for anything already paid or otherwise transferred by the consumer above the reduced amount.

(2) The amount of the reduction may, where appropriate, be the full amount of the price or whatever the consumer is required to transfer.

(3) Section 20(10) to (17) applies to a consumer's right to receive a refund under subsection (1)(b).

(4) The right to a price reduction does not apply—

(a) if what the consumer is (before the reduction) required to transfer under the contract, whether or not already transferred, cannot be divided up so as to enable the trader to receive or retain only the reduced amount, or

(b) if anything to which section 20(12) applies cannot be given back in its original state.

(5) A consumer who has the right to a price reduction and the final right to reject may only exercise one (not both), and may only do so in one of these situations—

(a) after one repair or one replacement, the goods do not conform to the contract;

(b) because of section 23(3) the consumer can require neither repair nor replacement of the goods; or

(c) the consumer has required the trader to repair or replace the goods, but the trader is in breach of the requirement of section 23(2)(a) to do so within a reasonable time and without significant inconvenience to the consumer.

(6) There has been a repair or replacement for the purposes of subsection (5)(a) if—

(a) the consumer has requested or agreed to repair or replacement of the goods (whether in relation to one fault or more than one), and

(b) the trader has delivered goods to the consumer, or made goods available to the consumer, in response to the request or agreement.

(7) For the purposes of subsection (6) goods that the trader arranges to repair at the consumer's premises are made available when the trader indicates that the repairs are finished.

(8) If the consumer exercises the final right to reject, any refund to the consumer may be reduced by a deduction for use, to take account of the use the consumer has had of the goods in the period since they were delivered, but this is subject to subsections (9) and (10).

(9) No deduction may be made to take account of use in any period when the consumer had the goods only because the trader failed to collect them at an agreed time.

(10) No deduction may be made if the final right to reject is exercised in the first 6 months (see subsection (11)), unless—

(a) the goods consist of a motor vehicle, or

(b) the goods are of a description specified by order made by the Secretary of State by statutory instrument.

(11) In subsection (10) the first 6 months means 6 months beginning with the first day after these have all happened—

(a) ownership or (in the case of a contract for the hire of goods, a hire-purchase agreement or a conditional sales contract) possession of the goods has been transferred to the consumer,

(b) the goods have been delivered, and

(c) where the contract requires the trader to install the goods or take other action to enable the consumer to use them, the trader has notified the consumer that the action has been taken.

(12) In subsection (10)(a) "motor vehicle"—

(a) in relation to Great Britain, has the same meaning as in the Road Traffic Act 1988 (see sections 185 to 194 of that Act);

(b) in relation to Northern Ireland, has the same meaning as in the Road Traffic (Northern Ireland) Order 1995 (SI 1995/2994 (NI 18)) (see Parts I and V of that Order).

(13) But a vehicle is not a motor vehicle for the purposes of subsection (10)(a) if it is constructed or adapted—

(a) for the use of a person suffering from some physical defect or disability, and

(b) so that it may only be used by one such person at any one time.

(14) An order under subsection (10)(b)—

(a) may be made only if the Secretary of State is satisfied that it is appropriate to do so because of significant detriment caused to traders as a result of the application of subsection (10) in relation to goods of the description specified by the order;

(b) may contain transitional or transitory provision or savings.

(15) No order may be made under subsection (10)(b) unless a draft of the statutory instrument containing it has been laid before, and approved by a resolution of, each House of Parliament.

Other rules about remedies under goods contracts

25 Delivery of wrong quantity

(1) Where the trader delivers to the consumer a quantity of goods less than the trader contracted to supply, the consumer may reject them, but if the consumer accepts them the consumer must pay for them at the contract rate.

(2) Where the trader delivers to the consumer a quantity of goods larger than the trader contracted to supply, the consumer may accept the goods included in the contract and reject the rest, or may reject all of the goods.

(3) Where the trader delivers to the consumer a quantity of goods larger than the trader contracted to supply and the consumer accepts all of the goods delivered, the consumer must pay for them at the contract rate.

(4) Where the consumer is entitled to reject goods under this section, any entitlement for the consumer to treat the contract as at an end depends on the terms of the contract and the circumstances of the case.

(5) The consumer rejects goods under this section by indicating to the trader that the consumer is rejecting the goods.

(6) The indication may be something the consumer says or does, but it must be clear enough to be understood by the trader.

(7) Subsections (1) to (3) do not prevent the consumer claiming damages, where it is open to the consumer to do so.

(8) This section is subject to any usage of trade, special agreement, or course of dealing between the parties.

26 Instalment deliveries

(1) Under a contract to supply goods, the consumer is not bound to accept delivery of the goods by instalments, unless that has been agreed between the consumer and the trader.

(2) The following provisions apply if the contract provides for the goods to be delivered by stated instalments, which are to be separately paid for.

(3) If the trader makes defective deliveries in respect of one or more instalments, the consumer, apart from any entitlement to claim damages, may be (but is not necessarily) entitled—
- (a) to exercise the short-term right to reject or the right to reject under section 19(6) (as applicable) in respect of the whole contract, or
- (b) to reject the goods in an instalment.

(4) Whether paragraph (a) or (b) of subsection (3) (or neither) applies to a consumer depends on the terms of the contract and the circumstances of the case.

(5) In subsection (3), making defective deliveries does not include failing to make a delivery in accordance with section 28.

(6) If the consumer neglects or refuses to take delivery of or pay for one or more instalments, the trader may—
- (a) be entitled to treat the whole contract as at an end, or
- (b) if it is a severable breach, have a claim for damages but not a right to treat the whole contract as at an end.

(7) Whether paragraph (a) or (b) of subsection (6) (or neither) applies to a trader depends on the terms of the contract and the circumstances of the case.

27 Consignation, or payment into court, in Scotland

(1) Subsection (2) applies where—
- (a) a consumer has not rejected goods which the consumer could have rejected for breach of a term mentioned in section 19(3) or (6),
- (b) the consumer has chosen to treat the breach as giving rise only to a claim for damages or to a right to rely on the breach against a claim by the trader for the price of the goods, and
- (c) the trader has begun proceedings in court to recover the price or has brought a counter-claim for the price.

(2) The court may require the consumer—
- (a) to consign, or pay into court, the price of the goods, or part of the price, or
- (b) to provide some other reasonable security for payment of the price.

Other rules about goods contracts

28 Delivery of goods

(1) This section applies to any sales contract.

(2) Unless the trader and the consumer have agreed otherwise, the contract is to be treated as including a term that the trader must deliver the goods to the consumer.

(3) Unless there is an agreed time or period, the contract is to be treated as including a term that the trader must deliver the goods—
- (a) without undue delay, and
- (b) in any event, not more than 30 days after the day on which the contract is entered into.

(4) In this section—

(a) an "agreed" time or period means a time or period agreed by the trader and the consumer for delivery of the goods;

(b) if there is an obligation to deliver the goods at the time the contract is entered into, that time counts as the "agreed" time.

(5) Subsections (6) and (7) apply if the trader does not deliver the goods in accordance with subsection (3) or at the agreed time or within the agreed period.

(6) If the circumstances are that—

(a) the trader has refused to deliver the goods,

(b) delivery of the goods at the agreed time or within the agreed period is essential taking into account all the relevant circumstances at the time the contract was entered into, or

(c) the consumer told the trader before the contract was entered into that delivery in accordance with subsection (3), or at the agreed time or within the agreed period, was essential,

then the consumer may treat the contract as at an end.

(7) In any other circumstances, the consumer may specify a period that is appropriate in the circumstances and require the trader to deliver the goods before the end of that period.

(8) If the consumer specifies a period under subsection (7) but the goods are not delivered within that period, then the consumer may treat the contract as at an end.

(9) If the consumer treats the contract as at an end under subsection (6) or (8), the trader must without undue delay reimburse all payments made under the contract.

(10) If subsection (6) or (8) applies but the consumer does not treat the contract as at an end—

(a) that does not prevent the consumer from cancelling the order for any of the goods or rejecting goods that have been delivered, and

(b) the trader must without undue delay reimburse all payments made under the contract in respect of any goods for which the consumer cancels the order or which the consumer rejects.

(11) If any of the goods form a commercial unit, the consumer cannot reject or cancel the order for some of those goods without also rejecting or cancelling the order for the rest of them.

(12) A unit is a "commercial unit" if division of the unit would materially impair the value of the goods or the character of the unit.

(13) This section does not prevent the consumer seeking other remedies where it is open to the consumer to do so.

(14) See section 2(5) and (6) for the application of this section where goods are sold at public auction.

29 Passing of risk

(1) A sales contract is to be treated as including the following provisions as terms.

(2) The goods remain at the trader's risk until they come into the physical possession of—

(a) the consumer, or

(b) a person identified by the consumer to take possession of the goods.

(3) Subsection (2) does not apply if the goods are delivered to a carrier who—

(a) is commissioned by the consumer to deliver the goods, and

(b) is not a carrier the trader named as an option for the consumer.

(4) In that case the goods are at the consumer's risk on and after delivery to the carrier.

(5) Subsection (4) does not affect any liability of the carrier to the consumer in respect of the goods.

(6) See section 2(5) and (6) for the application of this section where goods are sold at public auction.

30 Goods under guarantee

(1) This section applies where—

(a) there is a contract to supply goods, and

(b) there is a guarantee in relation to the goods.

(2) "Guarantee" here means an undertaking to the consumer given without extra charge by a person acting in the course of the person's business (the "guarantor") that, if the goods do not meet the specifications set out in the guarantee statement or in any associated advertising—

(a) the consumer will be reimbursed for the price paid for the goods, or

(b) the goods will be repaired, replaced or handled in any way.

(3) The guarantee takes effect, at the time the goods are delivered, as a contractual obligation owed by the guarantor under the conditions set out in the guarantee statement and in any associated advertising.

(4) The guarantor must ensure that—

(a) the guarantee sets out in plain and intelligible language the contents of the guarantee and the essential particulars for making claims under the guarantee,

(b) the guarantee states that the consumer has statutory rights in relation to the goods and that those rights are not affected by the guarantee, and

(c) where the goods are offered within the territory of the United Kingdom, the guarantee is written in English.

(5) The contents of the guarantee to be set out in it include, in particular—

(a) the name and address of the guarantor, and

(b) the duration and territorial scope of the guarantee.

(6) The guarantor and any other person who offers to supply to consumers the goods which are the subject of the guarantee must, on request by the consumer, make the guarantee available to the consumer within a reasonable time, in writing and in a form accessible to the consumer.

(7) What is a reasonable time is a question of fact.

(8) If a person fails to comply with a requirement of this section, the enforcement authority may apply to the court for an injunction or (in Scotland) an order of specific implement against that person requiring that person to comply.

(9) On an application the court may grant an injunction or (in Scotland) an order of specific implement on such terms as it thinks appropriate.

(10) In this section—

"court" means—

(a) in relation to England and Wales, the High Court or the county court,

(b) in relation to Northern Ireland, the High Court or a county court, and

(c) in relation to Scotland, the Court of Session or the sheriff;

"enforcement authority" means—

(a) the Competition and Markets Authority,

(b) a local weights and measures authority in Great Britain, and

(c) the Department of Enterprise, Trade and Investment in Northern Ireland.

Can a trader contract out of statutory rights and remedies under a goods contract?

31 Liability that cannot be excluded or restricted

(1) A term of a contract to supply goods is not binding on the consumer to the extent that it would exclude or restrict the trader's liability arising under any of these provisions—

(a) section 9 (goods to be of satisfactory quality);

(b) section 10 (goods to be fit for particular purpose);

(c) section 11 (goods to be as described);

(d) section 12 (other pre-contract information included in contract);

(e) section 13 (goods to match a sample);

(f) section 14 (goods to match a model seen or examined);

(g) section 15 (installation as part of conformity of the goods with the contract);

(h) section 16 (goods not conforming to contract if digital content does not conform);

(i) section 17 (trader to have right to supply the goods etc);

(j) section 28 (delivery of goods);

(k) section 29 (passing of risk).

(2) That also means that a term of a contract to supply goods is not binding on the consumer to the extent that it would—

(a) exclude or restrict a right or remedy in respect of a liability under a provision listed in subsection (1),

(b) make such a right or remedy or its enforcement subject to a restrictive or onerous condition,

(c) allow a trader to put a person at a disadvantage as a result of pursuing such a right or remedy, or

(d) exclude or restrict rules of evidence or procedure.

(3) The reference in subsection (1) to excluding or restricting a liability also includes preventing an obligation or duty arising or limiting its extent.

(4) An agreement in writing to submit present or future differences to arbitration is not to be regarded as excluding or restricting any liability for the purposes of this section.

(5) Subsection (1)(i), and subsection (2) so far as it relates to liability under section 17, do not apply to a term of a contract for the hire of goods.

(6) But an express term of a contract for the hire of goods is not binding on the consumer to the extent that it would exclude or restrict a term that section 17 requires to be treated as included in the contract, unless it is inconsistent with that term (and see also section 62 (requirement for terms to be fair)).

(7) See Schedule 3 for provision about the enforcement of this section.

32 Contracts applying law of non-EEA State

(1) If—

(a) the law of a country or territory other than an EEA State is chosen by the parties to be applicable to a sales contract, but

(b) the sales contract has a close connection with the United Kingdom,

this Chapter, except the provisions in subsection (2), applies despite that choice.

(2) The exceptions are—

(a) sections 11(4) and (5) and 12;

(b) sections 28 and 29;

(c) section 31(1)(d), (j) and (k).

(3) For cases where those provisions apply, or where the law applicable has not been chosen or the law of an EEA State is chosen, see Regulation (EC) No. 593/2008 of the European Parliament and of the Council of 17 June 2008 on the law applicable to contractual obligations.

CHAPTER 3

DIGITAL CONTENT

What digital content contracts are covered?

33 Contracts covered by this Chapter

(1) This Chapter applies to a contract for a trader to supply digital content to a consumer, if it is supplied or to be supplied for a price paid by the consumer.

(2) This Chapter also applies to a contract for a trader to supply digital content to a consumer, if—

(a) it is supplied free with goods or services or other digital content for which the consumer pays a price, and

(b) it is not generally available to consumers unless they have paid a price for it or for goods or services or other digital content.

(3) The references in subsections (1) and (2) to the consumer paying a price include references to the consumer using, by way of payment, any facility for which money has been paid.

(4) A trader does not supply digital content to a consumer for the purposes of this Part merely because the trader supplies a service by which digital content reaches the consumer.

(5) The Secretary of State may by order provide for this Chapter to apply to other contracts for a trader to supply digital content to a consumer, if the Secretary of State is satisfied that it is appropriate to do so because of significant detriment caused to consumers under contracts of the kind to which the order relates.

(6) An order under subsection (5)—

(a) may, in particular, amend this Act;

(b) may contain transitional or transitory provision or savings.

(7) A contract to which this Chapter applies is referred to in this Part as a "contract to supply digital content".

(8) This section, other than subsection (4), does not limit the application of section 46.

(9) The power to make an order under subsection (5) is exercisable by statutory instrument.

(10) No order may be made under subsection (5) unless a draft of the statutory instrument containing it has been laid before, and approved by a resolution of, each House of Parliament.

What statutory rights are there under a digital content contract?

34 Digital content to be of satisfactory quality

(1) Every contract to supply digital content is to be treated as including a term that the quality of the digital content is satisfactory.

(2) The quality of digital content is satisfactory if it meets the standard that a reasonable person would consider satisfactory, taking account of—

(a) any description of the digital content,

(b) the price mentioned in section 33(1) or (2)(b) (if relevant), and

(c) all the other relevant circumstances (see subsection (5)).

(3) The quality of digital content includes its state and condition; and the following aspects (among others) are in appropriate cases aspects of the quality of digital content—

(a) fitness for all the purposes for which digital content of that kind is usually supplied;

(b) freedom from minor defects;

(c) safety;

(d) durability.

(4) The term mentioned in subsection (1) does not cover anything which makes the quality of the digital content unsatisfactory—

(a) which is specifically drawn to the consumer's attention before the contract is made,
(b) where the consumer examines the digital content before the contract is made, which that examination ought to reveal, or
(c) where the consumer examines a trial version before the contract is made, which would have been apparent on a reasonable examination of the trial version.

(5) The relevant circumstances mentioned in subsection (2)(c) include any public statement about the specific characteristics of the digital content made by the trader, the producer or any representative of the trader or the producer.

(6) That includes, in particular, any public statement made in advertising or labelling.

(7) But a public statement is not a relevant circumstance for the purposes of subsection (2)(c) if the trader shows that—
(a) when the contract was made, the trader was not, and could not reasonably have been, aware of the statement,
(b) before the contract was made, the statement had been publicly withdrawn or, to the extent that it contained anything which was incorrect or misleading, it had been publicly corrected, or
(c) the consumer's decision to contract for the digital content could not have been influenced by the statement.

(8) In a contract to supply digital content a term about the quality of the digital content may be treated as included as a matter of custom.

(9) See section 42 for a consumer's rights if the trader is in breach of a term that this section requires to be treated as included in a contract.

35 Digital content to be fit for particular purpose

(1) Subsection (3) applies to a contract to supply digital content if before the contract is made the consumer makes known to the trader (expressly or by implication) any particular purpose for which the consumer is contracting for the digital content.

(2) Subsection (3) also applies to a contract to supply digital content if—
(a) the digital content was previously sold by a credit-broker to the trader,
(b) the consideration or part of it is a sum payable by instalments, and
(c) before the contract is made, the consumer makes known to the credit-broker (expressly or by implication) any particular purpose for which the consumer is contracting for the digital content.

(3) The contract is to be treated as including a term that the digital content is reasonably fit for that purpose, whether or not that is a purpose for which digital content of that kind is usually supplied.

(4) Subsection (3) does not apply if the circumstances show that the consumer does not rely, or it is unreasonable for the consumer to rely, on the skill or judgment of the trader or credit-broker.

(5) A contract to supply digital content may be treated as making provision about the fitness of the digital content for a particular purpose as a matter of custom.

(6) See section 42 for a consumer's rights if the trader is in breach of a term that this section requires to be treated as included in a contract.

36 Digital content to be as described

(1) Every contract to supply digital content is to be treated as including a term that the digital content will match any description of it given by the trader to the consumer.

(2) Where the consumer examines a trial version before the contract is made, it is not sufficient that the digital content matches (or is better than) the trial version if the digital content does not also match any description of it given by the trader to the consumer.

(3) Any information that is provided by the trader about the digital content that is information mentioned in paragraph (a), (j) or (k) of Schedule 1 or paragraph (a), (v) or (w) of Schedule 2 (main characteristics, functionality and compatibility) to the Consumer Contracts (Information, Cancellation and Additional Charges) Regulations 2013 (SI 2013/3134) is to be treated as included as a term of the contract.

(4) A change to any of that information, made before entering into the contract or later, is not effective unless expressly agreed between the consumer and the trader.

(5) See section 42 for a consumer's rights if the trader is in breach of a term that this section requires to be treated as included in a contract.

37 Other pre-contract information included in contract

(1) This section applies to any contract to supply digital content.

(2) Where regulation 9, 10 or 13 of the Consumer Contracts (Information, Cancellation and Additional Charges) Regulations 2013 (SI 2013/3134) required the trader to provide information to the consumer before the contract became binding, any of that information that was provided by the trader other than information about the digital content and mentioned in paragraph (a), (j) or (k) of Schedule 1 or paragraph (a), (v) or (w) of Schedule 2 to the Regulations (main characteristics, functionality and compatibility) is to be treated as included as a term of the contract.

(3) A change to any of that information, made before entering into the contract or later, is not effective unless expressly agreed between the consumer and the trader.

(4) See section 42 for a consumer's rights if the trader is in breach of a term that this section requires to be treated as included in a contract.

38 No other requirement to treat term about quality or fitness as included

(1) Except as provided by sections 34 and 35, a contract to supply digital content is not to be treated as including any term about the quality of the digital content or its fitness for any particular purpose, unless the term is expressly included in the contract.

(2) Subsection (1) is subject to provision made by any other enactment, whenever passed or made.

39 Supply by transmission and facilities for continued transmission

(1) Subsection (2) applies where there is a contract to supply digital content and the consumer's access to the content on a device requires its transmission to the device under arrangements initiated by the trader.

(2) For the purposes of this Chapter, the digital content is supplied—

(a) when the content reaches the device, or

(b) if earlier, when the content reaches another trader chosen by the consumer to supply, under a contract with the consumer, a service by which digital content reaches the device.

(3) Subsections (5) to (7) apply where—

(a) there is a contract to supply digital content, and

(b) after the trader (T) has supplied the digital content, the consumer is to have access under the contract to a processing facility under arrangements made by T.

(4) A processing facility is a facility by which T or another trader will receive digital content from the consumer and transmit digital content to the consumer (whether or not other features are to be included under the contract).

(5) The contract is to be treated as including a term that the processing facility (with any feature that the facility is to include under the contract) must be available to the consumer for a reasonable time, unless a time is specified in the contract.

(6) The following provisions apply to all digital content transmitted to the consumer on each occasion under the facility, while it is provided under the contract, as they apply to the digital content first supplied—

(a) section 34 (quality);

(b) section 35 (fitness for a particular purpose);

(c) section 36 (description).

(7) Breach of a term treated as included under subsection (5) has the same effect as breach of a term treated as included under those sections (see section 42).

40 Quality, fitness and description of content supplied subject to modifications

(1) Where under a contract a trader supplies digital content to a consumer subject to the right of the trader or a third party to modify the digital content, the following provisions apply in relation to the digital content as modified as they apply in relation to the digital content as supplied under the contract—

(a) section 34 (quality);

(b) section 35 (fitness for a particular purpose);

(c) section 36 (description).

(2) Subsection (1)(c) does not prevent the trader from improving the features of, or adding new features to, the digital content, as long as—

(a) the digital content continues to match the description of it given by the trader to the consumer, and

(b) the digital content continues to conform to the information provided by the trader as mentioned in subsection (3) of section 36, subject to any change to that information that has been agreed in accordance with subsection (4) of that section.

(3) A claim on the grounds that digital content does not conform to a term described in any of the sections listed in subsection (1) as applied by that subsection is to be treated as arising at the time when the digital content was supplied under the contract and not the time when it is modified.

41 Trader's right to supply digital content

(1) Every contract to supply digital content is to be treated as including a term—

(a) in relation to any digital content which is supplied under the contract and which the consumer has paid for, that the trader has the right to supply that content to the consumer;

(b) in relation to any digital content which the trader agrees to supply under the contract and which the consumer has paid for, that the trader will have the right to supply it to the consumer at the time when it is to be supplied.

(2) See section 42 for a consumer's rights if the trader is in breach of a term that this section requires to be treated as included in a contract.

What remedies are there if statutory rights under a digital content contract are not met?

42 Consumer's rights to enforce terms about digital content

(1) In this section and section 43 references to digital content conforming to a contract are references to the digital content conforming to the terms described in sections 34, 35 and 36.

(2) If the digital content does not conform to the contract, the consumer's rights (and the provisions about them and when they are available) are—

(a) the right to repair or replacement (see section 43);

(b) the right to a price reduction (see section 44).

(3) Section 16 also applies if an item including the digital content is supplied.

(4) If the trader is in breach of a term that section 37 requires to be treated as included in the contract, the consumer has the right to recover from the trader the amount of any costs incurred by the consumer as a result of the breach, up to the amount of the price paid for the digital content or for any facility within section 33(3) used by the consumer.

(5) If the trader is in breach of the term that section 41(1) (right to supply the content) requires to be treated as included in the contract, the consumer has the right to a refund (see section 45 for provisions about that right and when it is available).

(6) This Chapter does not prevent the consumer seeking other remedies for a breach of a term to which any of subsections (2), (4) or (5) applies, instead of or in addition to a remedy referred to there (but not so as to recover twice for the same loss).

(7) Those other remedies include any of the following that is open to the consumer in the circumstances—

(a) claiming damages;

(b) seeking to recover money paid where the consideration for payment of the money has failed;
(c) seeking specific performance;
(d) seeking an order for specific implement;
(e) relying on the breach against a claim by the trader for the price.

(8) It is not open to the consumer to treat the contract as at an end for breach of a term to which any of subsections (2), (4) or (5) applies.

(9) For the purposes of subsection (2), digital content which does not conform to the contract at any time within the period of six months beginning with the day on which it was supplied must be taken not to have conformed to the contract when it was supplied.

(10) Subsection (9) does not apply if—
(a) it is established that the digital content did conform to the contract when it was supplied, or
(b) its application is incompatible with the nature of the digital content or with how it fails to conform to the contract.

43 Right to repair or replacement

(1) This section applies if the consumer has the right to repair or replacement.

(2) If the consumer requires the trader to repair or replace the digital content, the trader must—
(a) do so within a reasonable time and without significant inconvenience to the consumer; and
(b) bear any necessary costs incurred in doing so (including in particular the cost of any labour, materials or postage).

(3) The consumer cannot require the trader to repair or replace the digital content if that remedy (the repair or the replacement)—
(a) is impossible, or
(b) is disproportionate compared to the other of those remedies.

(4) Either of those remedies is disproportionate compared to the other if it imposes costs on the trader which, compared to those imposed by the other, are unreasonable, taking into account—
(a) the value which the digital content would have if it conformed to the contract,
(b) the significance of the lack of conformity, and
(c) whether the other remedy could be effected without significant inconvenience to the consumer.

(5) Any question as to what is a reasonable time or significant inconvenience is to be determined taking account of—
(a) the nature of the digital content, and
(b) the purpose for which the digital content was obtained or accessed.

(6) A consumer who requires or agrees to the repair of digital content cannot require the trader to replace it without giving the trader a reasonable time to repair it (unless giving the trader that time would cause significant inconvenience to the consumer).

(7) A consumer who requires or agrees to the replacement of digital content cannot require the trader to repair it without giving the trader a reasonable time to replace it (unless giving the trader that time would cause significant inconvenience to the consumer).

(8) In this Chapter, "repair" in relation to digital content that does not conform to a contract, means making it conform.

44 Right to price reduction

(1) The right to a price reduction is the right to require the trader to reduce the price to the consumer by an appropriate amount (including the right to receive a refund for anything already paid above the reduced amount).

(2) The amount of the reduction may, where appropriate, be the full amount of the price.

(3) A consumer who has that right may only exercise it in one of these situations—

(a) because of section 43(3)(a) the consumer can require neither repair nor replacement of the digital content, or

(b) the consumer has required the trader to repair or replace the digital content, but the trader is in breach of the requirement of section 43(2)(a) to do so within a reasonable time and without significant inconvenience to the consumer.

(4) A refund under this section must be given without undue delay, and in any event within 14 days beginning with the day on which the trader agrees that the consumer is entitled to a refund.

(5) The trader must give the refund using the same means of payment as the consumer used to pay for the digital content, unless the consumer expressly agrees otherwise.

(6) The trader must not impose any fee on the consumer in respect of the refund.

45 Right to a refund

(1) The right to a refund gives the consumer the right to receive a refund from the trader of all money paid by the consumer for the digital content (subject to subsection (2)).

(2) If the breach giving the consumer the right to a refund affects only some of the digital content supplied under the contract, the right to a refund does not extend to any part of the price attributable to digital content that is not affected by the breach.

(3) A refund must be given without undue delay, and in any event within 14 days beginning with the day on which the trader agrees that the consumer is entitled to a refund.

(4) The trader must give the refund using the same means of payment as the consumer used to pay for the digital content, unless the consumer expressly agrees otherwise.

(5) The trader must not impose any fee on the consumer in respect of the refund.

Compensation for damage to device or to other digital content

46 Remedy for damage to device or to other digital content

(1) This section applies if—

(a) a trader supplies digital content to a consumer under a contract,
(b) the digital content causes damage to a device or to other digital content,
(c) the device or digital content that is damaged belongs to the consumer, and
(d) the damage is of a kind that would not have occurred if the trader had exercised reasonable care and skill.

(2) If the consumer requires the trader to provide a remedy under this section, the trader must either—
(a) repair the damage in accordance with subsection (3), or
(b) compensate the consumer for the damage with an appropriate payment.

(3) To repair the damage in accordance with this subsection, the trader must—
(a) repair the damage within a reasonable time and without significant inconvenience to the consumer, and
(b) bear any necessary costs incurred in repairing the damage (including in particular the cost of any labour, materials or postage).

(4) Any question as to what is a reasonable time or significant inconvenience is to be determined taking account of—
(a) the nature of the device or digital content that is damaged, and
(b) the purpose for which it is used by the consumer.

(5) A compensation payment under this section must be made without undue delay, and in any event within 14 days beginning with the day on which the trader agrees that the consumer is entitled to the payment.

(6) The trader must not impose any fee on the consumer in respect of the payment.

(7) A consumer with a right to a remedy under this section may bring a claim in civil proceedings to enforce that right.

(8) The Limitation Act 1980 and the Limitation (Northern Ireland) Order 1989 (SI 1989/1339 (NI 11)) apply to a claim under this section as if it were an action founded on simple contract.

(9) The Prescription and Limitation (Scotland) Act 1973 applies to a right to a remedy under this section as if it were an obligation to which section 6 of that Act applies.

Can a trader contract out of statutory rights and remedies under a digital content contract?

47 Liability that cannot be excluded or restricted

(1) A term of a contract to supply digital content is not binding on the consumer to the extent that it would exclude or restrict the trader's liability arising under any of these provisions—
(a) section 34 (digital content to be of satisfactory quality),
(b) section 35 (digital content to be fit for particular purpose),
(c) section 36 (digital content to be as described),
(d) section 37 (other pre-contract information included in contract), or
(e) section 41 (trader's right to supply digital content).

(2) That also means that a term of a contract to supply digital content is not binding on the consumer to the extent that it would—

(a) exclude or restrict a right or remedy in respect of a liability under a provision listed in subsection (1),

(b) make such a right or remedy or its enforcement subject to a restrictive or onerous condition,

(c) allow a trader to put a person at a disadvantage as a result of pursuing such a right or remedy, or

(d) exclude or restrict rules of evidence or procedure.

(3) The reference in subsection (1) to excluding or restricting a liability also includes preventing an obligation or duty arising or limiting its extent.

(4) An agreement in writing to submit present or future differences to arbitration is not to be regarded as excluding or restricting any liability for the purposes of this section.

(5) See Schedule 3 for provision about the enforcement of this section.

(6) For provision limiting the ability of a trader under a contract within section 46 to exclude or restrict the trader's liability under that section, see section 62.

CHAPTER 4

SERVICES

What services contracts are covered?

48 Contracts covered by this Chapter

(1) This Chapter applies to a contract for a trader to supply a service to a consumer.

(2) That does not include a contract of employment or apprenticeship.

(3) In relation to Scotland, this Chapter does not apply to a gratuitous contract.

(4) A contract to which this Chapter applies is referred to in this Part as a "contract to supply a service".

(5) The Secretary of State may by order made by statutory instrument provide that a provision of this Chapter does not apply in relation to a service of a description specified in the order.

(6) The power in subsection (5) includes power to provide that a provision of this Chapter does not apply in relation to a service of a description specified in the order in the circumstances so specified.

(7) An order under subsection (5) may contain transitional or transitory provision or savings.

(8) No order may be made under subsection (5) unless a draft of the statutory instrument containing it has been laid before, and approved by a resolution of, each House of Parliament.

What statutory rights are there under a services contract?

49 Service to be performed with reasonable care and skill

(1) Every contract to supply a service is to be treated as including a term that the trader must perform the service with reasonable care and skill.

(2) See section 54 for a consumer's rights if the trader is in breach of a term that this section requires to be treated as included in a contract.

50 Information about the trader or service to be binding

(1) Every contract to supply a service is to be treated as including as a term of the contract anything that is said or written to the consumer, by or on behalf of the trader, about the trader or the service, if—

- (a) it is taken into account by the consumer when deciding to enter into the contract, or
- (b) it is taken into account by the consumer when making any decision about the service after entering into the contract.

(2) Anything taken into account by the consumer as mentioned in subsection (1)(a) or (b) is subject to—

- (a) anything that qualified it and was said or written to the consumer by the trader on the same occasion, and
- (b) any change to it that has been expressly agreed between the consumer and the trader (before entering into the contract or later).

(3) Without prejudice to subsection (1), any information provided by the trader in accordance with regulation 9, 10 or 13 of the Consumer Contracts (Information, Cancellation and Additional Charges) Regulations 2013 (SI 2013/3134) is to be treated as included as a term of the contract.

(4) A change to any of the information mentioned in subsection (3), made before entering into the contract or later, is not effective unless expressly agreed between the consumer and the trader.

(5) See section 54 for a consumer's rights if the trader is in breach of a term that this section requires to be treated as included in a contract.

51 Reasonable price to be paid for a service

(1) This section applies to a contract to supply a service if—

- (a) the consumer has not paid a price or other consideration for the service,
- (b) the contract does not expressly fix a price or other consideration, and does not say how it is to be fixed, and
- (c) anything that is to be treated under section 50 as included in the contract does not fix a price or other consideration either.

(2) In that case the contract is to be treated as including a term that the consumer must pay a reasonable price for the service, and no more.

(3) What is a reasonable price is a question of fact.

52 Service to be performed within a reasonable time

(1) This section applies to a contract to supply a service, if—

(a) the contract does not expressly fix the time for the service to be performed, and does not say how it is to be fixed, and

(b) information that is to be treated under section 50 as included in the contract does not fix the time either.

(2) In that case the contract is to be treated as including a term that the trader must perform the service within a reasonable time.

(3) What is a reasonable time is a question of fact.

(4) See section 54 for a consumer's rights if the trader is in breach of a term that this section requires to be treated as included in a contract.

53 Relation to other law on contract terms

(1) Nothing in this Chapter affects any enactment or rule of law that imposes a stricter duty on the trader.

(2) This Chapter is subject to any other enactment which defines or restricts the rights, duties or liabilities arising in connection with a service of any description.

What remedies are there if statutory rights under a services contract are not met?

54 Consumer's rights to enforce terms about services

(1) The consumer's rights under this section and sections 55 and 56 do not affect any rights that the contract provides for, if those are not inconsistent.

(2) In this section and section 55 a reference to a service conforming to a contract is a reference to—

(a) the service being performed in accordance with section 49, or

(b) the service conforming to a term that section 50 requires to be treated as included in the contract and that relates to the performance of the service.

(3) If the service does not conform to the contract, the consumer's rights (and the provisions about them and when they are available) are—

(a) the right to require repeat performance (see section 55);

(b) the right to a price reduction (see section 56).

(4) If the trader is in breach of a term that section 50 requires to be treated as included in the contract but that does not relate to the service, the consumer has the right to a price reduction (see section 56 for provisions about that right and when it is available).

(5) If the trader is in breach of what the contract requires under section 52 (performance within a reasonable time), the consumer has the right to a price reduction (see section 56 for provisions about that right and when it is available).

(6) This section and sections 55 and 56 do not prevent the consumer seeking other remedies for a breach of a term to which any of subsections (3) to (5) applies, instead of or in addition to a remedy referred to there (but not so as to recover twice for the same loss).

(7) Those other remedies include any of the following that is open to the consumer in the circumstances—
(a) claiming damages;
(b) seeking to recover money paid where the consideration for payment of the money has failed;
(c) seeking specific performance;
(d) seeking an order for specific implement;
(e) relying on the breach against a claim by the trader under the contract;
(f) exercising a right to treat the contract as at an end.

55 Right to repeat performance

(1) The right to require repeat performance is a right to require the trader to perform the service again, to the extent necessary to complete its performance in conformity with the contract.

(2) If the consumer requires such repeat performance, the trader—
(a) must provide it within a reasonable time and without significant inconvenience to the consumer; and
(b) must bear any necessary costs incurred in doing so (including in particular the cost of any labour or materials).

(3) The consumer cannot require repeat performance if completing performance of the service in conformity with the contract is impossible.

(4) Any question as to what is a reasonable time or significant inconvenience is to be determined taking account of—
(a) the nature of the service, and
(b) the purpose for which the service was to be performed.

56 Right to price reduction

(1) The right to a price reduction is the right to require the trader to reduce the price to the consumer by an appropriate amount (including the right to receive a refund for anything already paid above the reduced amount).

(2) The amount of the reduction may, where appropriate, be the full amount of the price.

(3) A consumer who has that right and the right to require repeat performance is only entitled to a price reduction in one of these situations—
(a) because of section 55(3) the consumer cannot require repeat performance; or
(b) the consumer has required repeat performance, but the trader is in breach of the requirement of section 55(2)(a) to do it within a reasonable time and without significant inconvenience to the consumer.

(4) A refund under this section must be given without undue delay, and in any event within 14 days beginning with the day on which the trader agrees that the consumer is entitled to a refund.

(5) The trader must give the refund using the same means of payment as the consumer used to pay for the service, unless the consumer expressly agrees otherwise.

(6) The trader must not impose any fee on the consumer in respect of the refund.

Can a trader contract out of statutory rights and remedies under a services contract?

57 Liability that cannot be excluded or restricted

(1) A term of a contract to supply services is not binding on the consumer to the extent that it would exclude the trader's liability arising under section 49 (service to be performed with reasonable care and skill).

(2) Subject to section 50(2), a term of a contract to supply services is not binding on the consumer to the extent that it would exclude the trader's liability arising under section 50 (information about trader or service to be binding).

(3) A term of a contract to supply services is not binding on the consumer to the extent that it would restrict the trader's liability arising under any of sections 49 and 50 and, where they apply, sections 51 and 52 (reasonable price and reasonable time), if it would prevent the consumer in an appropriate case from recovering the price paid or the value of any other consideration. (If it would not prevent the consumer from doing so, Part 2 (unfair terms) may apply.)

(4) That also means that a term of a contract to supply services is not binding on the consumer to the extent that it would —

(a) exclude or restrict a right or remedy in respect of a liability under any of sections 49 to 52,

(b) make such a right or remedy or its enforcement subject to a restrictive or onerous condition,

(c) allow a trader to put a person at a disadvantage as a result of pursuing such a right or remedy, or

(d) exclude or restrict rules of evidence or procedure.

(5) The references in subsections (1) to (3) to excluding or restricting a liability also include preventing an obligation or duty arising or limiting its extent.

(6) An agreement in writing to submit present or future differences to arbitration is not to be regarded as excluding or restricting any liability for the purposes of this section.

(7) See Schedule 3 for provision about the enforcement of this section.

CHAPTER 5

GENERAL AND SUPPLEMENTARY PROVISIONS

58 Powers of the court

(1) In any proceedings in which a remedy is sought by virtue of section 19(3) or (4), 42(2) or 54(3), the court, in addition to any other power it has, may act under this section.

(2) On the application of the consumer the court may make an order requiring specific performance or, in Scotland, specific implement by the trader of any obligation imposed on the trader by virtue of section 23, 43 or 55.

(3) Subsection (4) applies if—

(a) the consumer claims to exercise a right under the relevant remedies provisions, but

(b) the court decides that those provisions have the effect that exercise of another right is appropriate.

(4) The court may proceed as if the consumer had exercised that other right.

(5) If the consumer has claimed to exercise the final right to reject, the court may order that any reimbursement to the consumer is reduced by a deduction for use, to take account of the use the consumer has had of the goods in the period since they were delivered.

(6) Any deduction for use is limited as set out in section 24(9) and (10).

(7) The court may make an order under this section unconditionally or on such terms and conditions as to damages, payment of the price and otherwise as it thinks just.

(8) The "relevant remedies provisions" are—

(a) where Chapter 2 applies, sections 23 and 24;

(b) where Chapter 3 applies, sections 43 and 44;

(c) where Chapter 4 applies, sections 55 and 56.

59 Interpretation

(1) These definitions apply in this Part (as well as the key definitions in section 2)—

"conditional sales contract" has the meaning given in section 5(3);

"Consumer Rights Directive" means Directive 2011/83/EU of the European Parliament and of the Council of 25 October 2011 on consumer rights, amending Council Directive 93/13/EEC and Directive 1999/44/EC of the European Parliament and of the Council and repealing Council Directive 85/577/EEC and Directive 97/7/EC of the European Parliament and of the Council;

"credit-broker" means a person acting in the course of a business of credit brokerage carried on by that person;

"credit brokerage" means—

(a) introducing individuals who want to obtain credit to persons carrying on any business so far as it relates to the provision of credit,

(b) introducing individuals who want to obtain goods on hire to persons carrying on a business which comprises or relates to supplying goods under a contract for the hire of goods, or

(c) introducing individuals who want to obtain credit, or to obtain goods on hire, to other persons engaged in credit brokerage;

"delivery" means voluntary transfer of possession from one person to another;

"enactment" includes—

(a) an enactment contained in subordinate legislation within the meaning of the Interpretation Act 1978,

(b) an enactment contained in, or in an instrument made under, a Measure or Act of the National Assembly for Wales,

(c) an enactment contained in, or in an instrument made under, an Act of the Scottish Parliament, and

(d) an enactment contained in, or in an instrument made under, Northern Ireland legislation;

"producer", in relation to goods or digital content, means—

(a) the manufacturer,

(b) the importer into the European Economic Area, or

(c) any person who purports to be a producer by placing the person's name, trade mark or other distinctive sign on the goods or using it in connection with the digital content.

(2) References in this Part to treating a contract as at an end are to be read in accordance with section 19(13).

60 Changes to other legislation

Schedule 1 (amendments consequential on this Part) has effect.

PART 2

UNFAIR TERMS

What contracts and notices are covered by this Part?

61 Contracts and notices covered by this Part

(1) This Part applies to a contract between a trader and a consumer.

(2) This does not include a contract of employment or apprenticeship.

(3) A contract to which this Part applies is referred to in this Part as a "consumer contract".

(4) This Part applies to a notice to the extent that it—

(a) relates to rights or obligations as between a trader and a consumer, or

(b) purports to exclude or restrict a trader's liability to a consumer.

(5) This does not include a notice relating to rights, obligations or liabilities as between an employer and an employee.

(6) It does not matter for the purposes of subsection (4) whether the notice is expressed to apply to a consumer, as long as it is reasonable to assume it is intended to be seen or heard by a consumer.

(7) A notice to which this Part applies is referred to in this Part as a "consumer notice".

(8) In this section "notice" includes an announcement, whether or not in writing, and any other communication or purported communication.

What are the general rules about fairness of contract terms and notices?

62 Requirement for contract terms and notices to be fair

(1) An unfair term of a consumer contract is not binding on the consumer.

(2) An unfair consumer notice is not binding on the consumer.

(3) This does not prevent the consumer from relying on the term or notice if the consumer chooses to do so.

(4) A term is unfair if, contrary to the requirement of good faith, it causes a significant imbalance in the parties' rights and obligations under the contract to the detriment of the consumer.

(5) Whether a term is fair is to be determined—
   (a) taking into account the nature of the subject matter of the contract, and
   (b) by reference to all the circumstances existing when the term was agreed and to all of the other terms of the contract or of any other contract on which it depends.

(6) A notice is unfair if, contrary to the requirement of good faith, it causes a significant imbalance in the parties' rights and obligations to the detriment of the consumer.

(7) Whether a notice is fair is to be determined—
   (a) taking into account the nature of the subject matter of the notice, and
   (b) by reference to all the circumstances existing when the rights or obligations to which it relates arose and to the terms of any contract on which it depends.

(8) This section does not affect the operation of—
   (a) section 31 (exclusion of liability: goods contracts),
   (b) section 47 (exclusion of liability: digital content contracts),
   (c) section 57 (exclusion of liability: services contracts), or
   (d) section 65 (exclusion of negligence liability).

63 Contract terms which may or must be regarded as unfair

(1) Part 1 of Schedule 2 contains an indicative and non-exhaustive list of terms of consumer contracts that may be regarded as unfair for the purposes of this Part.

(2) Part 1 of Schedule 2 is subject to Part 2 of that Schedule; but a term listed in Part 2 of that Schedule may nevertheless be assessed for fairness under section 62 unless section 64 or 73 applies to it.

(3) The Secretary of State may by order made by statutory instrument amend Schedule 2 so as to add, modify or remove an entry in Part 1 or Part 2 of that Schedule.

(4) An order under subsection (3) may contain transitional or transitory provision or savings.

(5) No order may be made under subsection (3) unless a draft of the statutory instrument containing it has been laid before, and approved by a resolution of, each House of Parliament.

(6) A term of a consumer contract must be regarded as unfair if it has the effect that the consumer bears the burden of proof with respect to compliance by a distance supplier or an intermediary with an obligation under any enactment or rule implementing the Distance Marketing Directive.

(7) In subsection (6)—

"the Distance Marketing Directive" means Directive 2002/65/EC of the European Parliament and of the Council of 23 September 2002 concerning the distance marketing of consumer financial services and amending Council Directive 90/619/EEC and Directives 97/7/EC and 98/27/EC;

"distance supplier" means—

(a) a supplier under a distance contract within the meaning of the Financial Services (Distance Marketing) Regulations 2004 (SI 2004/2095), or

(b) a supplier of unsolicited financial services within the meaning of regulation 15 of those regulations;

"enactment" includes an enactment contained in subordinate legislation within the meaning of the Interpretation Act 1978;

"intermediary" has the same meaning as in the Financial Services (Distance Marketing) Regulations 2004;

"rule" means a rule made by the Financial Conduct Authority or the Prudential Regulation Authority under the Financial Services and Markets Act 2000 or by a designated professional body within the meaning of section 326(2) of that Act.

64 Exclusion from assessment of fairness

(1) A term of a consumer contract may not be assessed for fairness under section 62 to the extent that—

(a) it specifies the main subject matter of the contract, or

(b) the assessment is of the appropriateness of the price payable under the contract by comparison with the goods, digital content or services supplied under it.

(2) Subsection (1) excludes a term from an assessment under section 62 only if it is transparent and prominent.

(3) A term is transparent for the purposes of this Part if it is expressed in plain and intelligible language and (in the case of a written term) is legible.

(4) A term is prominent for the purposes of this section if it is brought to the consumer's attention in such a way that an average consumer would be aware of the term.

(5) In subsection (4) "average consumer" means a consumer who is reasonably well-informed, observant and circumspect.

(6) This section does not apply to a term of a contract listed in Part 1 of Schedule 2.

65 Bar on exclusion or restriction of negligence liability

(1) A trader cannot by a term of a consumer contract or by a consumer notice exclude or restrict liability for death or personal injury resulting from negligence.

(2) Where a term of a consumer contract, or a consumer notice, purports to exclude or restrict a trader's liability for negligence, a person is not to be taken to have voluntarily accepted any risk merely because the person agreed to or knew about the term or notice.

(3) In this section "personal injury" includes any disease and any impairment of physical or mental condition.

(4) In this section "negligence" means the breach of—

(a) any obligation to take reasonable care or exercise reasonable skill in the performance of a contract where the obligation arises from an express or implied term of the contract,

(b) a common law duty to take reasonable care or exercise reasonable skill,

(c) the common duty of care imposed by the Occupiers' Liability Act 1957 or the Occupiers' Liability Act (Northern Ireland) 1957, or

(d) the duty of reasonable care imposed by section 2(1) of the Occupiers' Liability (Scotland) Act 1960.

(5) It is immaterial for the purposes of subsection (4)—

(a) whether a breach of duty or obligation was inadvertent or intentional, or

(b) whether liability for it arises directly or vicariously.

(6) This section is subject to section 66 (which makes provision about the scope of this section).

66 Scope of section 65

(1) Section 65 does not apply to—

(a) any contract so far as it is a contract of insurance, including a contract to pay an annuity on human life, or

(b) any contract so far as it relates to the creation or transfer of an interest in land.

(2) Section 65 does not affect the validity of any discharge or indemnity given by a person in consideration of the receipt by that person of compensation in settlement of any claim the person has.

(3) Section 65 does not—

(a) apply to liability which is excluded or discharged as mentioned in section 4(2)(a) (exception to liability to pay damages to relatives) of the Damages (Scotland) Act 2011, or

(b) affect the operation of section 5 (discharge of liability to pay damages: exception for mesothelioma) of that Act.

(4) Section 65 does not apply to the liability of an occupier of premises to a person who obtains access to the premises for recreational purposes if—

(a) the person suffers loss or damage because of the dangerous state of the premises, and

(b) allowing the person access for those purposes is not within the purposes of the occupier's trade, business, craft or profession.

67 Effect of an unfair term on the rest of a contract

Where a term of a consumer contract is not binding on the consumer as a result of this Part, the contract continues, so far as practicable, to have effect in every other respect.

68 Requirement for transparency

(1) A trader must ensure that a written term of a consumer contract, or a consumer notice in writing, is transparent.

(2) A consumer notice is transparent for the purposes of subsection (1) if it is expressed in plain and intelligible language and it is legible.

69 Contract terms that may have different meanings

(1) If a term in a consumer contract, or a consumer notice, could have different meanings, the meaning that is most favourable to the consumer is to prevail.

(2) Subsection (1) does not apply to the construction of a term or a notice in proceedings on an application for an injunction or interdict under paragraph 3 of Schedule 3.

How are the general rules enforced?

70 Enforcement of the law on unfair contract terms

(1) Schedule 3 confers functions on the Competition and Markets Authority and other regulators in relation to the enforcement of this Part.

(2) For provision about the investigatory powers that are available to those regulators for the purposes of that Schedule, see Schedule 5.

Supplementary provisions

71 Duty of court to consider fairness of term

(1) Subsection (2) applies to proceedings before a court which relate to a term of a consumer contract.

(2) The court must consider whether the term is fair even if none of the parties to the proceedings has raised that issue or indicated that it intends to raise it.

(3) But subsection (2) does not apply unless the court considers that it has before it sufficient legal and factual material to enable it to consider the fairness of the term.

72 Application of rules to secondary contracts

(1) This section applies if a term of a contract ("the secondary contract") reduces the rights or remedies or increases the obligations of a person under another contract ("the main contract").

(2) The term is subject to the provisions of this Part that would apply to the term if it were in the main contract.

(3) It does not matter for the purposes of this section—

- (a) whether the parties to the secondary contract are the same as the parties to the main contract, or
- (b) whether the secondary contract is a consumer contract.

(4) This section does not apply if the secondary contract is a settlement of a claim arising under the main contract.

73 Disapplication of rules to mandatory terms and notices

(1) This Part does not apply to a term of a contract, or to a notice, to the extent that it reflects—

(a) mandatory statutory or regulatory provisions, or

(b) the provisions or principles of an international convention to which the United Kingdom or the EU is a party.

(2) In subsection (1) "mandatory statutory or regulatory provisions" includes rules which, according to law, apply between the parties on the basis that no other arrangements have been established.

74 Contracts applying law of non-EEA State

(1) If—

(a) the law of a country or territory other than an EEA State is chosen by the parties to be applicable to a consumer contract, but

(b) the consumer contract has a close connection with the United Kingdom,

this Part applies despite that choice.

(2) For cases where the law applicable has not been chosen or the law of an EEA State is chosen, see Regulation (EC) No. 593/2008 of the European Parliament and of the Council of 17 June 2008 on the law applicable to contractual obligations.

75 Changes to other legislation

Schedule 4 (amendments consequential on this Part) has effect.

76 Interpretation of Part 2

(1) In this Part—

"consumer contract" has the meaning given by section 61(3);

"consumer notice" has the meaning given by section 61(7);

"transparent" is to be construed in accordance with sections 64(3) and 68(2).

(2) The following have the same meanings in this Part as they have in Part 1—

"trader" (see section 2(2));

"consumer" (see section 2(3));

"goods" (see section 2(8));

"digital content" (see section 2(9)).

(3) Section 2(4) (trader who claims an individual is not a consumer must prove it) applies in relation to this Part as it applies in relation to Part 1.

PART 3

MISCELLANEOUS AND GENERAL

CHAPTER 1

ENFORCEMENT ETC.

77 Investigatory powers etc

(1) Schedule 5 (investigatory powers etc) has effect.

(2) Schedule 6 (investigatory powers: consequential amendments) has effect.

78 Amendment of weights and measures legislation regarding unwrapped bread

(1) In the Weights and Measures (Packaged Goods) Regulations 2006 (S.I. 2006/659), Schedule 5 (application to bread) is amended in accordance with subsections (2) and (3).

(2) For paragraph 9 substitute—

"9 Regulation 9(1)(b)(ii) (duty to keep records) does not apply to bread which is sold unwrapped or in open packs."

(3) After paragraph 13 insert—

"14 (1) Regulation 9(1)(b)(ii) (duty to keep records) does not apply to a packer who holds a notice of exemption which is in force.

(2) A "notice of exemption" means a notice issued under paragraph 9 as it stood before section 78 of the Consumer Rights Act 2015 came into force."

(4) The use of this Act to make amendments to the Weights and Measures (Packaged Goods) Regulations 2006 has no effect on the availability of any power in the Weights and Measures Act 1985 to amend or revoke those Regulations, including the provision substituted by subsection (2) and that inserted by subsection (3).

(5) In the Weights and Measures (Packaged Goods) Regulations (Northern Ireland) 2011 (SR 2011/331), Schedule 5 (application to bread) is amended in accordance with subsections (6) and (7).

(6) For paragraph 9 substitute—

"9 Regulation 9(1)(b)(ii) (duty to keep records) does not apply to bread which is sold unwrapped or in open packets."

(7) After paragraph 13 insert—

"14 (1) Regulation 9(1)(b)(ii) (duty to keep records) does not apply to a packer who holds a notice of exemption which is in force.

(2) A "notice of exemption" means a notice issued under paragraph 9 as it stood before section 78 of the Consumer Rights Act 2015 came into force."

(8) The use of this Act to make amendments to the Weights and Measures (Packaged Goods) Regulations (Northern Ireland) 2011 has no effect on the availability of any power in the Weights and Measures (Northern Ireland) Order 1981 (SI 1981/231 (NI 10)) to amend or revoke those Regulations, including the provision substituted by subsection (6) and that inserted by subsection (7).

79 Enterprise Act 2002: enhanced consumer measures and other enforcement

(1) Schedule 7 contains amendments of Part 8 of the Enterprise Act 2002 (enforcement of certain consumer legislation).

(2) The amendments have effect only in relation to conduct which occurs, or which is likely to occur, after the commencement of this section.

80 Contravention of code regulating premium rate services

(1) In section 120(3) of the Communications Act 2003 (conditions under section 120 must require compliance with directions given in accordance with an approved code or with an order under section 122) before paragraph (a) insert—

"(za) the provisions of an approved code;".

(2) In section 121(5) of that Act (provision about enforcement that may be made by approved code) after paragraph (a) insert—

"(aa) provision that applies where there is or has been more than one contravention of the code or directions given in accordance with it by a person and which enables—

(i) a single penalty (which does not exceed that maximum penalty) to be imposed on the person in respect of all of those contraventions, or

(ii) separate penalties (each of which does not exceed that maximum penalty) to be imposed on the person in respect of each of those contraventions,

according to whether the person imposing the penalty determines that a single penalty or separate penalties are appropriate and proportionate to those contraventions;".

(3) Section 123 of that Act (enforcement by OFCOM of conditions under section 120) is amended as follows.

(4) After subsection (1) insert—

"(1A) Subsection (1B) applies where a notification under section 94 as applied by this section relates to more than one contravention of—

(a) a code approved under section 121,

(b) directions given in accordance with such a code, or

(c) an order under section 122.

(1B) Section 96(3) as applied by this section enables OFCOM to impose—

(a) a single penalty in respect of all of those contraventions, or

(b) separate penalties in respect of each of those contraventions,

according to whether OFCOM determine that a single penalty or separate penalties are appropriate and proportionate to those contraventions."

(5) In subsection (2) (maximum amount of penalty) for "the penalty" substitute "each penalty".

CHAPTER 2

COMPETITION

81 Private actions in competition law

Schedule 8 (private actions in competition law) has effect.

82 Appointment of judges to the Competition Appeal Tribunal

(1) In section 12(2) of the Enterprise Act 2002 (constitution of the Competition Appeal Tribunal) after paragraph (a) insert—

"(aa) such judges as are nominated from time to time by the Lord Chief Justice of England and Wales from the High Court of England and Wales;

(ab) such judges as are nominated from time to time by the Lord President of the Court of Session from the judges of the Court of Session;

(ac) such judges as are nominated from time to time by the Lord Chief Justice of Northern Ireland from the High Court in Northern Ireland;".

(2) In section 14 of that Act (constitution of the Competition Appeal Tribunal for particular proceedings and its decisions)—

(a) in subsection (2) after "the President" insert ", a judge within any of paragraphs (aa) to (ac) of section 12(2)", and

(b) in subsection (3) for "either" substitute "the judges within paragraphs (aa) to (ac) of section 12(2),".

(3) In Schedule 4 (Tribunal procedure) to that Act, in paragraph 18(3)(b) (consequences of member of Tribunal being unable to continue) after "if that person is not" insert "a judge within any of paragraphs (aa) to (ac) of section 12(2) or".

CHAPTER 3

DUTY OF LETTING AGENTS TO PUBLICISE FEES ETC

83 Duty of letting agents to publicise fees etc

(1) A letting agent must, in accordance with this section, publicise details of the agent's relevant fees.

(2) The agent must display a list of the fees—

(a) at each of the agent's premises at which the agent deals face-to-face with persons using or proposing to use services to which the fees relate, and

(b) at a place in each of those premises at which the list is likely to be seen by such persons.

(3) The agent must publish a list of the fees on the agent's website (if it has a website).

(4) A list of fees displayed or published in accordance with subsection (2) or (3) must include—

(a) a description of each fee that is sufficient to enable a person who is liable to pay it to understand the service or cost that is covered by the fee or the purpose for which it is imposed (as the case may be),

(b) in the case of a fee which tenants are liable to pay, an indication of whether the fee relates to each dwelling-house or each tenant under a tenancy of the dwelling-house, and

(c) the amount of each fee inclusive of any applicable tax or, where the amount of a fee cannot reasonably be determined in advance, a description of how that fee is calculated.

(5) Subsections (6) and (7) apply to a letting agent engaging in letting agency or property management work in relation to dwelling-houses in England.

(6) If the agent holds money on behalf of persons to whom the agent provides services as part of that work, the duty imposed on the agent by subsection (2) or (3) includes a duty to display or publish, with the list of fees, a statement of whether the agent is a member of a client money protection scheme.

(7) If the agent is required to be a member of a redress scheme for dealing with complaints in connection with that work, the duty imposed on the agent by subsection (2) or (3) includes a duty to display or publish, with the list of fees, a statement—

(a) that indicates that the agent is a member of a redress scheme, and

(b) that gives the name of the scheme.

(8) The appropriate national authority may by regulations specify—

(a) other ways in which a letting agent must publicise details of the relevant fees charged by the agent or (where applicable) a statement within subsection (6) or (7);

(b) the details that must be given of fees publicised in that way.

(9) In this section—

"client money protection scheme" means a scheme which enables a person on whose behalf a letting agent holds money to be compensated if all or part of that money is not repaid to that person in circumstances where the scheme applies;

"redress scheme" means a redress scheme for which provision is made by order under section 83 or 84 of the Enterprise and Regulatory Reform Act 2013.

84 Letting agents to which the duty applies

(1) In this Chapter "letting agent" means a person who engages in letting agency work (whether or not that person engages in other work).

(2) A person is not a letting agent for the purposes of this Chapter if the person engages in letting agency work in the course of that person's employment under a contract of employment.

(3) A person is not a letting agent for the purposes of this Chapter if—

(a) the person is of a description specified in regulations made by the appropriate national authority;

(b) the person engages in work of a description specified in regulations made by the appropriate national authority.

85 Fees to which the duty applies

(1) In this Chapter "relevant fees", in relation to a letting agent, means the fees, charges or penalties (however expressed) payable to the agent by a landlord or tenant—

(a) in respect of letting agency work carried on by the agent,

(b) in respect of property management work carried on by the agent, or

(c) otherwise in connection with—

(i) an assured tenancy of a dwelling-house, or

(ii) a dwelling-house that is, has been or is proposed to be let under an assured tenancy.

(2) Subsection (1) does not apply to—

(a) the rent payable to a landlord under a tenancy,

(b) any fees, charges or penalties which the letting agent receives from a landlord under a tenancy on behalf of another person,

(c) a tenancy deposit within the meaning of section 212(8) of the Housing Act 2004, or

(d) any fees, charges or penalties of a description specified in regulations made by the appropriate national authority.

86 Letting agency work and property management work

(1) In this Chapter "letting agency work" means things done by a person in the course of a business in response to instructions received from—

(a) a person ("a prospective landlord") seeking to find another person wishing to rent a dwelling-house under an assured tenancy and, having found such a person, to grant such a tenancy, or

(b) a person ("a prospective tenant") seeking to find a dwelling-house to rent under an assured tenancy and, having found such a dwelling-house, to obtain such a tenancy of it.

(2) But "letting agency work" does not include any of the following things when done by a person who does nothing else within subsection (1)—

(a) publishing advertisements or disseminating information;

(b) providing a means by which a prospective landlord or a prospective tenant can, in response to an advertisement or dissemination of information, make direct contact with a prospective tenant or a prospective landlord;

(c) providing a means by which a prospective landlord and a prospective tenant can communicate directly with each other.

(3) "Letting agency work" also does not include things done by a local authority.

(4) In this Chapter "property management work", in relation to a letting agent, means things done by the agent in the course of a business in response to instructions received from another person where—

(a) that person wishes the agent to arrange services, repairs, maintenance, improvements or insurance in respect of, or to deal with any other aspect of the management of, premises on the person's behalf, and

(b) the premises consist of a dwelling-house let under an assured tenancy.

87 Enforcement of the duty

(1) It is the duty of every local weights and measures authority in England and Wales to enforce the provisions of this Chapter in its area.

(2) If a letting agent breaches the duty in section 83(3) (duty to publish list of fees etc on agent's website), that breach is taken to have occurred in each area of a local weights and measures authority in England and Wales in which a dwelling-house to which the fees relate is located.

(3) Where a local weights and measures authority in England and Wales is satisfied on the balance of probabilities that a letting agent has breached a duty imposed by or under section 83, the authority may impose a financial penalty on the agent in respect of that breach.

(4) A local weights and measures authority in England and Wales may impose a penalty under this section in respect of a breach which occurs in England and Wales but outside that authority's area (as well as in respect of a breach which occurs within that area).

(5) But a local weights and measures authority in England and Wales may impose a penalty in respect of a breach which occurs outside its area and in the area of a local weights and measures authority in Wales only if it has obtained the consent of that authority.

(6) Only one penalty under this section may be imposed on the same letting agent in respect of the same breach.

(7) The amount of a financial penalty imposed under this section—

(a) may be such as the authority imposing it determines, but

(b) must not exceed £5,000.

(8) Schedule 9 (procedure for and appeals against financial penalties) has effect.

(9) A local weights and measures authority in England must have regard to any guidance issued by the Secretary of State about—

(a) compliance by letting agents with duties imposed by or under section 83;

(b) the exercise of its functions under this section or Schedule 9.

(10) A local weights and measures authority in Wales must have regard to any guidance issued by the Welsh Ministers about—

(a) compliance by letting agents with duties imposed by or under section 83;

(b) the exercise of its functions under this section or Schedule 9.

(11) The Secretary of State may by regulations made by statutory instrument—

(a) amend any of the provisions of this section or Schedule 9 in their application in relation to local weights and measures authorities in England;

(b) make consequential amendments to Schedule 5 in its application in relation to such authorities.

(12) The Welsh Ministers may by regulations made by statutory instrument—

(a) amend any of the provisions of this section or Schedule 9 in their application in relation to local weights and measures authorities in Wales;

(b) make consequential amendments to Schedule 5 in its application in relation to such authorities.

88 Supplementary provisions

(1) In this Chapter—

"the appropriate national authority" means—

(a) in relation to England, the Secretary of State, and

(b) in relation to Wales, the Welsh Ministers;

"assured tenancy" means a tenancy which is an assured tenancy for the purposes of the Housing Act 1988 except where—

(a) the landlord is—

(i) a private registered provider of social housing,

(ii) a registered social landlord, or

(iii) a fully mutual housing association, or

(b) the tenancy is a long lease;

"dwelling-house" may be a house or part of a house;

"fully mutual housing association" has the same meaning as in Part 1 of the Housing Associations Act 1985 (see section 1(1) and (2) of that Act);

"landlord" includes a person who proposes to be a landlord under a tenancy and a person who has ceased to be a landlord under a tenancy because the tenancy has come to an end;

"long lease" means a lease which—

(a) is a long lease for the purposes of Chapter 1 of Part 1 of the Leasehold Reform, Housing and Urban Development Act 1993, or

(b) in the case of a shared ownership lease (within the meaning given by section 7(7) of that Act), would be a lease within paragraph (a) of this definition if the tenant's total share (within the meaning given by that section) were 100%;

"registered social landlord" means a body registered as a social landlord under Chapter 1 of Part 1 of the Housing Act 1996;

"tenant" includes a person who proposes to be a tenant under a tenancy and a person who has ceased to be a tenant under a tenancy because the tenancy has come to an end.

(2) In this Chapter "local authority" means—

(a) a county council,

(b) a county borough council,

(c) a district council,

(d) a London borough council,

(e) the Common Council of the City of London in its capacity as local authority, or

(f) the Council of the Isles of Scilly.

(3) References in this Chapter to a tenancy include a proposed tenancy and a tenancy that has come to an end.

(4) References in this Chapter to anything which is payable, or which a person is liable to pay, to a letting agent include anything that the letting agent claims a person is liable to pay, regardless of whether the person is in fact liable to pay it.

(5) Regulations under this Chapter are to be made by statutory instrument.

(6) A statutory instrument containing (whether alone or with other provision) regulations made by the Secretary of State under section 87(11) is not to be made unless a draft of the instrument has been laid before, and approved by a resolution of, each House of Parliament.

(7) A statutory instrument containing (whether alone or with other provision) regulations made by the Welsh Ministers under section 87(12) is not to be made unless a draft of the instrument has been laid before, and approved by a resolution of, the National Assembly for Wales.

(8) A statutory instrument containing regulations made by the Secretary of State under this Chapter other than one to which subsection (6) applies is subject to annulment in pursuance of a resolution of either House of Parliament.

(9) A statutory instrument containing regulations made by the Welsh Ministers under this Chapter other than one to which subsection (7) applies is subject to annulment in pursuance of a resolution of the National Assembly for Wales.

(10) Regulations under this Chapter—

(a) may make different provision for different purposes;

(b) may make provision generally or in relation to specific cases.

(11) Regulations under this Chapter may include incidental, supplementary, consequential, transitional, transitory or saving provision.

CHAPTER 4

STUDENT COMPLAINTS SCHEME

89 Qualifying institutions for the purposes of the student complaints scheme

(1) The Higher Education Act 2004 is amended as follows.

(2) In section 11 (qualifying institutions for the purposes of the student complaints scheme) after paragraph (d) insert—

"(e) an institution (other than one within another paragraph of this section) which provides higher education courses which are designated for the purposes of section 22 of the 1998 Act by or under regulations under that section;

(f) an institution (other than one within another paragraph of this section) whose entitlement to grant awards is conferred by an order under section 76(1) of the 1992 Act."

(3) In section 12 (qualifying complaints for the purposes of the student complaints scheme)—

(a) in subsection (1) for "subsection (2)" substitute "subsections (2) and (3)", and

(b) after subsection (2) insert—

"(3) The designated operator may determine that a complaint within subsection (1) about an act or omission of a qualifying institution within paragraph (e) or (f) of section 11 is a qualifying complaint only if it is made by a person who is undertaking or has undertaken a particular course or a course of a particular description."

CHAPTER 5

SECONDARY TICKETING

90 Duty to provide information about tickets

(1) This section applies where a person ("the seller") re-sells a ticket for a recreational, sporting or cultural event in the United Kingdom through a secondary ticketing facility.

(2) The seller and each operator of the facility must ensure that the person who buys the ticket ("the buyer") is given the information specified in subsection (3), where this is applicable to the ticket.

(3) That information is—

(a) where the ticket is for a particular seat or standing area at the venue for the event, the information necessary to enable the buyer to identify that seat or standing area,

(b) information about any restriction which limits use of the ticket to persons of a particular description, and

(c) the face value of the ticket.

(4) The reference in subsection (3)(a) to information necessary to enable the buyer to identify a seat or standing area at a venue includes, so far as applicable—

(a) the name of the area in the venue in which the seat or standing area is located (for example the name of the stand in which it is located),

(b) information necessary to enable the buyer to identify the part of the area in the venue in which the seat or standing area is located (for example the block of seats in which the seat is located),

(c) the number, letter or other distinguishing mark of the row in which the seat is located, and

(d) the number, letter or other distinguishing mark of the seat.

(5) The reference in subsection (3)(c) to the face value of the ticket is to the amount stated on the ticket as its price.

(6) The seller and each operator of the facility must ensure that the buyer is given the information specified in subsection (7), where the seller is—

(a) an operator of the secondary ticketing facility,

(b) a person who is a parent undertaking or a subsidiary undertaking in relation to an operator of the secondary ticketing facility,

(c) a person who is employed or engaged by an operator of the secondary ticketing facility,

(d) a person who is acting on behalf of a person within paragraph (c), or

(e) an organiser of the event or a person acting on behalf of an organiser of the event.

(7) That information is a statement that the seller of the ticket is a person within subsection (6) which specifies the ground on which the seller falls within that subsection.

(8) Information required by this section to be given to the buyer must be given—

(a) in a clear and comprehensible manner, and

(b) before the buyer is bound by the contract for the sale of the ticket.

(9) This section applies in relation to the re-sale of a ticket through a secondary ticketing facility only if the ticket is first offered for re-sale through the facility after the coming into force of this section.

91 Prohibition on cancellation or blacklisting

(1) This section applies where a person ("the seller") re-sells, or offers for re-sale, a ticket for a recreational, sporting or cultural event in the United Kingdom through a secondary ticketing facility.

(2) An organiser of the event must not cancel the ticket merely because the seller has re-sold the ticket or offered it for re-sale unless—

(a) a term of the original contract for the sale of the ticket—

(i) provided for its cancellation if it was re-sold by the buyer under that contract,

(ii) provided for its cancellation if it was offered for re-sale by that buyer, or

(iii) provided as mentioned in sub-paragraph (i) and (ii), and

(b) that term was not unfair for the purposes of Part 2 (unfair terms).

(3) An organiser of the event must not blacklist the seller merely because the seller has re-sold the ticket or offered it for re-sale unless—

(a) a term of the original contract for the sale of the ticket—

(i) provided for the blacklisting of the buyer under that contract if it was re-sold by that buyer,

(ii) provided for the blacklisting of that buyer if it was offered for re-sale by that buyer, or

(iii) provided as mentioned in sub-paragraph (i) and (ii), and

(b) that term was not unfair for the purposes of Part 2 (unfair terms).

(4) In subsections (2) and (3) "the original contract" means the contract for the sale of the ticket by an organiser of the event to a person other than an organiser of the event.

(5) For the purposes of this section an organiser of an event cancels a ticket if the organiser takes steps which result in the holder for the time being of the ticket no longer being entitled to attend that event.

(6) For the purposes of this section an organiser of an event blacklists a person if the organiser takes steps—

(a) to prevent the person from acquiring a ticket for a recreational, sporting or cultural event in the United Kingdom, or

(b) to restrict the person's opportunity to acquire such a ticket.

(7) Part 2 (unfair terms) may apply to a term of a contract which, apart from that Part, would permit the cancellation of a ticket for a recreational, sporting or cultural event in the United Kingdom, or the blacklisting of the seller of such a ticket, in circumstances other than those mentioned in subsection (2) or (3).

(8) Before the coming into force of Part 2, references to that Part in this section are to be read as references to the Unfair Terms in Consumer Contracts Regulations 1999 (SI 1999/2083).

(9) This section applies in relation to a ticket that is re-sold or offered for re-sale before or after the coming into force of this section; but the prohibition in this section applies only to things done after its coming into force.

92 Duty to report criminal activity

(1) This section applies where—

(a) an operator of a secondary ticketing facility knows that a person has used or is using the facility in such a way that an offence has been or is being committed, and

(b) the offence relates to the re-sale of a ticket for a recreational, sporting or cultural event in the United Kingdom.

(2) The operator must, as soon as the operator becomes aware that a person has used or is using the facility as mentioned in subsection (1), disclose the matters specified in subsection (3) to—

(a) an appropriate person, and

(b) an organiser of the event (subject to subsection (5)).

(3) Those matters are—

(a) the identity of the person mentioned in subsection (1), if this is known to the operator, and

(b) the fact that the operator knows that an offence has been or is being committed as mentioned in that subsection.

(4) The following are appropriate persons for the purposes of this section—

(a) a constable of a police force in England and Wales,

(b) a constable of the police service of Scotland, and

(c) a police officer within the meaning of the Police (Northern Ireland) Act 2000.

(5) This section does not require an operator to make a disclosure to an organiser of an event if the operator has reasonable grounds for believing that to do so will prejudice the investigation of any offence.

(6) References in this section to an offence are to an offence under the law of any part of the United Kingdom.

(7) This section applies only in relation to an offence of which an operator becomes aware after the coming into force of this section.

93 Enforcement of this Chapter

(1) A local weights and measures authority in Great Britain may enforce the provisions of this Chapter in its area.

(2) The Department of Enterprise, Trade and Investment may enforce the provisions of this Chapter in Northern Ireland.

(3) Each of the bodies referred to in subsections (1) and (2) is an "enforcement authority" for the purposes of this Chapter.

(4) Where an enforcement authority is satisfied on the balance of probabilities that a person has breached a duty or prohibition imposed by this Chapter, the authority may impose a financial penalty on the person in respect of that breach.

(5) But in the case of a breach of a duty in section 90 or a prohibition in section 91 an enforcement authority may not impose a financial penalty on a person ("P") if the authority is satisfied on the balance of probabilities that—

(a) the breach was due to—

(i) a mistake,

(ii) reliance on information supplied to P by another person,

(iii) the act or default of another person,

(iv) an accident, or

(v) another cause beyond P's control, and

(b) P took all reasonable precautions and exercised all due diligence to avoid the breach.

(6) A local weights and measures authority in England and Wales may impose a penalty under this section in respect of a breach which occurs in England and Wales but outside that authority's area (as well as in respect of a breach which occurs within that area).

(7) A local weights and measures authority in Scotland may impose a penalty under this section in respect of a breach which occurs in Scotland but outside that authority's area (as well as in respect of a breach which occurs within that area).

(8) Only one penalty under this section may be imposed on the same person in respect of the same breach.

(9) The amount of a financial penalty imposed under this section—

(a) may be such as the enforcement authority imposing it determines, but

(b) must not exceed £5,000.

(10) Schedule 10 (procedure for and appeals against financial penalties) has effect.

(11) References in this section to this Chapter do not include section 94.

94 Duty to review measures relating to secondary ticketing

(1) The Secretary of State must—

(a) review, or arrange for a review of, consumer protection measures applying to the re-sale of tickets for recreational, sporting or cultural events in the United Kingdom through secondary ticketing facilities,

(b) prepare a report on the outcome of the review or arrange for such a report to be prepared, and

(c) publish that report.

(2) The report must be published before the end of the period of 12 months beginning with the day on which this section comes into force.

(3) The Secretary of State must lay the report before Parliament.

(4) In this section "consumer protection measures" includes such legislation, rules of law, codes of practice and guidance as the Secretary of State considers relate to the rights of consumers or the protection of their interests.

95 Interpretation of this Chapter

(1) In this Chapter—

"enforcement authority" has the meaning given by section 93(3);

"operator", in relation to a secondary ticketing facility, means a person who—

(a) exercises control over the operation of the facility, and

(b) receives revenue from the facility,

but this is subject to regulations under subsection (2);

"organiser", in relation to an event, means a person who—

(a) is responsible for organising or managing the event, or

(b) receives some or all of the revenue from the event;

"parent undertaking" has the meaning given by section 1162 of the Companies Act 2006;

"secondary ticketing facility" means an internet-based facility for the re-sale of tickets for recreational, sporting or cultural events;

"subsidiary undertaking" has the meaning given by section 1162 of the Companies Act 2006;

"undertaking" has the meaning given by section 1161(1) of the Companies Act 2006.

(2) The Secretary of State may by regulations provide that a person of a description specified in the regulations is or is not to be treated for the purposes of this Chapter as an operator in relation to a secondary ticketing facility.

(3) Regulations under subsection (2)—

(a) are to be made by statutory instrument;

(b) may make different provision for different purposes;

(c) may include incidental, supplementary, consequential, transitional, transitory or saving provision.

(4) A statutory instrument containing regulations under subsection (2) is not to be made unless a draft of the instrument has been laid before, and approved by a resolution of, each House of Parliament.

CHAPTER 6

GENERAL

96 Power to make consequential provision

(1) The Secretary of State may by order made by statutory instrument make provision in consequence of this Act.

(2) The power conferred by subsection (1) includes power—

(a) to amend, repeal, revoke or otherwise modify any provision made by an enactment or an instrument made under an enactment (including an enactment passed or instrument made in the same Session as this Act);

(b) to make transitional, transitory or saving provision.

(3) A statutory instrument containing (whether alone or with other provision) an order under this section which amends, repeals, revokes or otherwise modifies any provision of primary legislation is not to be made unless a draft of the instrument has been laid before, and approved by a resolution of, each House of Parliament.

(4) A statutory instrument containing an order under this section which does not amend, repeal, revoke or otherwise modify any provision of primary legislation is subject to annulment in pursuance of a resolution of either House of Parliament.

(5) In this section—

"enactment" includes an Act of the Scottish Parliament, a Measure or Act of the National Assembly for Wales and Northern Ireland legislation;

"primary legislation" means—

(a) an Act of Parliament,

(b) an Act of the Scottish Parliament,

(c) a Measure or Act of the National Assembly for Wales, and

(d) Northern Ireland legislation.

97 Power to make transitional, transitory and saving provision

(1) The Secretary of State may by order made by statutory instrument make transitional, transitory or saving provision in connection with the coming into force of any provision of this Act other than the coming into force of Chapter 3 or 4 of this Part in relation to Wales.

(2) The Welsh Ministers may by order made by statutory instrument make transitional, transitory or saving provision in connection with the coming into force of Chapter 3 or 4 of this Part in relation to Wales.

98 Financial provision

There is to be paid out of money provided by Parliament—

(a) any expenses incurred by a Minister of the Crown or a government department under this Act, and

(b) any increase attributable to this Act in the sums payable under any other Act out of money so provided.

99 Extent

(1) The amendment, repeal or revocation of any provision by this Act has the same extent as the provision concerned.

(2) Section 27 extends only to Scotland.

(3) Chapter 3 of this Part extends only to England and Wales.

(4) Subject to that, this Act extends to England and Wales, Scotland and Northern Ireland.

100 Commencement

(1) The provisions of this Act listed in subsection (2) come into force on the day on which this Act is passed.

(2) Those provisions are—

(a) section 48(5) to (8),

(b) Chapter 3 of this Part in so far as it confer powers to make regulations,

(c) section 88(5) to (11),

(d) this Chapter, and

(e) paragraph 12 of Schedule 5.

(3) Chapters 3 and 4 of this Part come into force—

(a) in relation to England, on such day as the Secretary of State may appoint by order made by statutory instrument;

(b) in relation to Wales, on such day as the Welsh Ministers may appoint by order made by statutory instrument.

(4) Chapter 5 of this Part comes into force at the end of the period of two months beginning with the day on which this Act is passed.

(5) The other provisions of this Act come into force on such day as the Secretary of State may appoint by order made by statutory instrument.

(6) An order under this section may appoint different days for different purposes.

101 Short title

This Act may be cited as the Consumer Rights Act 2015.

SCHEDULES

SCHEDULE 1

Section 60

AMENDMENTS CONSEQUENTIAL ON PART 1

Supply of Goods (Implied Terms) Act 1973 (c. 13)

1 The Supply of Goods (Implied Terms) Act 1973 is amended as follows.

2 For "hire-purchase agreement" (or "hire purchase agreement") in each place, except in section 15(1), substitute "relevant hire-purchase agreement".

3 (1) Section 10 (implied undertakings as to quality or fitness) is amended as follows.

(2) Omit subsections (2D) to (2F).

(3) Omit subsection (8).

4 (1) Section 11A (modification of remedies for breach of statutory condition in non-consumer cases) is amended as follows.

(2) In subsection (1) omit "then, if the person to whom the goods are bailed does not deal as consumer,".

(3) In subsection (3), for paragraph (b) substitute—

"(b) that the agreement was a relevant hire-purchase agreement."

(4) Omit subsection (4).

5 In section 12A (remedies for breach of hire-purchase agreement as respects Scotland) omit subsections (2) and (3).

6 Omit section 14 (special provisions as to conditional sale agreements).

7 (1) Section 15 (supplementary) is amended as follows.

(2) In subsection (1)—

(a) in the definition of "hire-purchase agreement" at the end insert—

"and a hire-purchase agreement is relevant if it is not a contract to which Chapter 2 of Part 1 of the Consumer Rights Act 2015 applies;", and

(b) omit the definition of "producer".

(3) Omit subsection (3).

Sale of Goods Act 1979 (c. 54)

8 The Sale of Goods Act 1979 is amended as follows.

9 In section 1 (contracts to which Act applies), after subsection (4) insert—

"(5) Certain sections or subsections of this Act do not apply to a contract to which Chapter 2 of Part 1 of the Consumer Rights Act 2015 applies.

(6) Where that is the case it is indicated in the section concerned."

10 In section 11 (when condition to be treated as warranty), after subsection (4) insert—

"(4A) Subsection (4) does not apply to a contract to which Chapter 2 of Part 1 of the Consumer Rights Act 2015 applies (but see the provision made about such contracts in sections 19 to 22 of that Act)."

11 In section 12 (implied terms about title etc), after subsection (6) insert—

"(7) This section does not apply to a contract to which Chapter 2 of Part 1 of the Consumer Rights Act 2015 applies (but see the provision made about such contracts in section 17 of that Act)."

12 In section 13 (sale by description), after subsection (4) insert—

"(5) This section does not apply to a contract to which Chapter 2 of Part 1 of the Consumer Rights Act 2015 applies (but see the provision made about such contracts in section 11 of that Act)."

13 (1) Section 14 (implied terms about quality or fitness) is amended as follows.

(2) Omit subsections (2D) to (2F).

(3) After subsection (8) insert—

"(9) This section does not apply to a contract to which Chapter 2 of Part 1 of the Consumer Rights Act 2015 applies (but see the provision made about such contracts in sections 9, 10 and 18 of that Act)."

14 In section 15 (sale by sample), after subsection (4) insert—

"(5) This section does not apply to a contract to which Chapter 2 of Part 1 of the Consumer Rights Act 2015 applies (but see the provision made about such contracts in sections 13 and 18 of that Act)."

15 In section 15A (modification of remedies for breach of condition in non-consumer cases), in subsection (1) omit "then, if the buyer does not deal as consumer,".

16 (1) Section 15B (remedies for breach of contract as respects Scotland) is amended as follows.

(2) After subsection (1) insert—

"(1A) Subsection (1) does not apply to a contract to which Chapter 2 of Part 1 of the Consumer Rights Act 2015 applies (but see the provision made about such contracts in sections 19 to 22 of that Act)."

(3) Omit subsection (2).

17 (1) In section 20 (passing of risk), for subsection (4) substitute—

"(4) This section does not apply to a contract to which Chapter 2 of Part 1 of the Consumer Rights Act 2015 applies (but see the provision made about such contracts in section 29 of that Act)."

(2) The marginal note "Passing of risk" substituted by the Sale and Supply of Goods to Consumers Regulations 2002 (SI 2002/3045) is not affected by the revocation of those Regulations by this Schedule.

18 In section 29 (rules about delivery), after subsection (3) insert—

"(3A) Subsection (3) does not apply to a contract to which Chapter 2 of Part 1 of the Consumer Rights Act 2015 applies (but see the provision made about such contracts in section 28 of that Act)."

19 (1) Section 30 (delivery of wrong quantity) is amended as follows.

(2) In subsection (2A) omit "who does not deal as consumer".

(3) After subsection (5) insert—

"(6) This section does not apply to a contract to which Chapter 2 of Part 1 of the Consumer Rights Act 2015 applies (but see the provision made about such contracts in section 25 of that Act)."

20 In section 31 (instalment deliveries) after subsection (2) insert—

"(3) This section does not apply to a contract to which Chapter 2 of Part 1 of the Consumer Rights Act 2015 applies (but see the provision made about such contracts in section 26 of that Act)."

21 In section 32 (delivery to carrier), for subsection (4) substitute—

"(4) This section does not apply to a contract to which Chapter 2 of Part 1 of the Consumer Rights Act 2015 applies (but see the provision made about such contracts in section 29 of that Act)."

22 (1) Section 33 (risk where goods are delivered at distant place) is amended as follows.

(2) At the beginning insert "(1)".

(3) At the end insert—

"(2) This section does not apply to a contract to which Chapter 2 of Part 1 of the Consumer Rights Act 2015 applies (but see the provision made about such contracts in section 29 of that Act)."

23 (1) Section 34 (buyer's right of examining the goods) is amended as follows.

(2) At the beginning insert "(1)".

(3) At the end insert—

"(2) Nothing in this section affects the operation of section 22 (time limit for short-term right to reject) of the Consumer Rights Act 2015."

24 (1) Section 35 (acceptance) is amended as follows.

(2) Omit subsection (3).

(3) After subsection (8) insert—

"(9) This section does not apply to a contract to which Chapter 2 of Part 1 of the Consumer Rights Act 2015 applies (but see the provision made about such contracts in section 21 of that Act)."

25 In section 35A (right of partial rejection), after subsection (4) insert—

"(5) This section does not apply to a contract to which Chapter 2 of Part 1 of the Consumer Rights Act 2015 applies (but see the provision made about such contracts in section 21 of that Act)."

26 (1) Section 36 (buyer not bound to return rejected goods) is amended as follows.

(2) At the beginning insert "(1)".

(3) At the end insert—

"(2) This section does not apply to a contract to which Chapter 2 of Part 1 of the Consumer Rights Act 2015 applies (but see the provision made about such contracts in section 20 of that Act)."

27 Omit Part 5A (additional rights of buyer in consumer cases).

28 In section 51 (damages for non-delivery), after subsection (3) insert—

"(4) This section does not apply to a contract to which Chapter 2 of Part 1 of the Consumer Rights Act 2015 applies (but see the provision made about such contracts in section 19 of that Act)."

29 In section 52 (specific performance), after subsection (4) insert—

"(5) This section does not apply to a contract to which Chapter 2 of Part 1 of the Consumer Rights Act 2015 applies (but see the provision made about such contracts in section 19 of that Act)."

30 In section 53 (remedy for breach of warranty), after subsection (4) insert—

"(4A) This section does not apply to a contract to which Chapter 2 of Part 1 of the Consumer Rights Act 2015 applies (but see the provision made about such contracts in section 19 of that Act)."

31 In section 53A (measure of damages as respects Scotland), after subsection (2) insert—

"(2A) This section does not apply to a contract to which Chapter 2 of Part 1 of the Consumer Rights Act 2015 applies (but see the provision made about such contracts in section 19 of that Act)."

32 (1) Section 54 (interest) is amended as follows.

(2) At the beginning insert "(1)".

(3) At the end insert—

"(2) This section does not apply to a contract to which Chapter 2 of Part 1 of the Consumer Rights Act 2015 applies (but see the provision made about such contracts in section 19 of that Act)."

33 In section 55 (exclusion of implied terms), after subsection (1) insert—

"(1A) Subsection (1) does not apply to a contract to which Chapter 2 of Part 1 of the Consumer Rights Act 2015 applies (but see the provision made about such contracts in section 31 of that Act)."

34 (1) Section 58 (payment into court in Scotland) is amended as follows.

(2) At the beginning insert "(1)".

(3) At the end insert—

"(2) This section does not apply to a contract to which Chapter 2 of Part 1 of the Consumer Rights Act 2015 applies (but see the provision made about such contracts in section 27 of that Act)."

35 (1) Section 61 (interpretation) is amended as follows.

(2) In subsection (1) omit the following definitions—

(a) "consumer contract";

(b) "producer";

(c) "repair".

(3) Omit subsection (5A).

36 In section 62(2) (savings for rules of law etc), for "this Act" substitute "legislation including this Act and the Consumer Rights Act 2015".

Supply of Goods and Services Act 1982 (c. 29)

37 The Supply of Goods and Services Act 1982 is amended as follows.

38 In each place—

(a) for "contract for the transfer of goods" substitute "relevant contract for the transfer of goods";

(b) for "contract for the hire of goods" substitute "relevant contract for the hire of goods";

(c) for "contract for the supply of a service" substitute "relevant contract for the supply of a service".

39 In section 1 (the contracts concerned: transfer of property in goods, as respects England and Wales and Northern Ireland), in subsection (1) at the end insert ", and other than a contract to which Chapter 2 of Part 1 of the Consumer Rights Act 2015 applies."

40 In section 4 (implied terms about quality or fitness in contracts for transfer of goods) omit subsections (2B) to (2D).

41 In section 5A (modification of remedies for breach of statutory condition in non-consumer cases), in subsection (1) omit "then, if the transferee does not deal as consumer,".

42 In section 6 (the contracts concerned: hire of goods, as respects England and Wales and Northern Ireland), in subsection (1) at the end insert ", and other than a contract to which Chapter 2 of Part 1 of the Consumer Rights Act 2015 applies."

43 In section 9 (implied terms about quality or fitness in contracts for hire of goods) omit subsections (2B) to (2D).

44 In section 10A (modification of remedies for breach of statutory condition in non-consumer cases) in subsection (1) omit "then, if the bailee does not deal as consumer,".

45 In section 11A (the contracts concerned: transfer of property in goods, as respects Scotland), in subsection (1) at the end insert ", and other than a contract to which Chapter 2 of Part 1 of the Consumer Rights Act 2015 applies."

46 In section 11D (implied terms about quality or fitness in contracts for transfer of property in goods) omit subsections (3A) to (3C) and (10).

47 In section 11F (remedies for breach of contract) omit subsections (2) and (3).

48 In section 11G (the contracts concerned: hire of goods, as respects Scotland), in subsection (1) at the end insert ", and other than a contract to which Chapter 2 of Part 1 of the Consumer Rights Act 2015 applies."

49 In section 11J (implied terms about quality or fitness in contracts for hire of goods) omit subsections (3A) to (3C) and (10).

50 Omit Part 1B (additional rights of transferee in consumer cases).

51 In section 12 (the contracts concerned: supply of services, as respects England and Wales and Northern Ireland), in subsection (1) at the end insert ", other than a contract to which Chapter 4 of Part 1 of the Consumer Rights Act 2015 applies."

52 (1) Section 18 (interpretation: general) is amended as follows.

(2) In subsection (1) omit the definitions of "producer" and "repair".

(3) Omit subsection (4).

Sale and Supply of Goods to Consumers Regulations 2002 (SI 2002/3045)

53 The Sale and Supply of Goods to Consumers Regulations 2002 are revoked.

Regulatory Enforcement and Sanctions Act 2008 (c. 13)

54 In Schedule 3 to the Regulatory Enforcement and Sanctions Act 2008 (enactments specified for the purposes of Part 1), at the appropriate place insert—

"Consumer Rights Act 2015, Part 1".

Consequential repeal and revocation

55 In consequence of the amendments made by this Schedule—

(a) omit paragraph 5(9) of Schedule 2 to the Sale and Supply of Goods Act 1994, and

(b) omit paragraph 97 of Schedule 2 to the Consumer Protection from Unfair Trading Regulations 2008 (SI 2008/1277).

SCHEDULE 2

Section 63

CONSUMER CONTRACT TERMS WHICH MAY BE REGARDED AS UNFAIR

PART 1

LIST OF TERMS

1 A term which has the object or effect of excluding or limiting the trader's liability in the event of the death of or personal injury to the consumer resulting from an act or omission of the trader.

2 A term which has the object or effect of inappropriately excluding or limiting the legal rights of the consumer in relation to the trader or another party in the event

of total or partial non-performance or inadequate performance by the trader of any of the contractual obligations, including the option of offsetting a debt owed to the trader against any claim which the consumer may have against the trader.

3 A term which has the object or effect of making an agreement binding on the consumer in a case where the provision of services by the trader is subject to a condition whose realisation depends on the trader's will alone.

4 A term which has the object or effect of permitting the trader to retain sums paid by the consumer where the consumer decides not to conclude or perform the contract, without providing for the consumer to receive compensation of an equivalent amount from the trader where the trader is the party cancelling the contract.

5 A term which has the object or effect of requiring that, where the consumer decides not to conclude or perform the contract, the consumer must pay the trader a disproportionately high sum in compensation or for services which have not been supplied.

6 A term which has the object or effect of requiring a consumer who fails to fulfil his obligations under the contract to pay a disproportionately high sum in compensation.

7 A term which has the object or effect of authorising the trader to dissolve the contract on a discretionary basis where the same facility is not granted to the consumer, or permitting the trader to retain the sums paid for services not yet supplied by the trader where it is the trader who dissolves the contract.

8 A term which has the object or effect of enabling the trader to terminate a contract of indeterminate duration without reasonable notice except where there are serious grounds for doing so.

9 A term which has the object or effect of automatically extending a contract of fixed duration where the consumer does not indicate otherwise, when the deadline fixed for the consumer to express a desire not to extend the contract is unreasonably early.

10 A term which has the object or effect of irrevocably binding the consumer to terms with which the consumer has had no real opportunity of becoming acquainted before the conclusion of the contract.

11 A term which has the object or effect of enabling the trader to alter the terms of the contract unilaterally without a valid reason which is specified in the contract.

12 A term which has the object or effect of permitting the trader to determine the characteristics of the subject matter of the contract after the consumer has become bound by it.

13 A term which has the object or effect of enabling the trader to alter unilaterally without a valid reason any characteristics of the goods, digital content or services to be provided.

14 A term which has the object or effect of giving the trader the discretion to decide the price payable under the contract after the consumer has become bound by it, where no price or method of determining the price is agreed when the consumer becomes bound.

15 A term which has the object or effect of permitting a trader to increase the price of goods, digital content or services without giving the consumer the right to cancel the contract if the final price is too high in relation to the price agreed when the contract was concluded.

16 A term which has the object or effect of giving the trader the right to determine whether the goods, digital content or services supplied are in conformity with the contract, or giving the trader the exclusive right to interpret any term of the contract.

17 A term which has the object or effect of limiting the trader's obligation to respect commitments undertaken by the trader's agents or making the trader's commitments subject to compliance with a particular formality.

18 A term which has the object or effect of obliging the consumer to fulfil all of the consumer's obligations where the trader does not perform the trader's obligations.

19 A term which has the object or effect of allowing the trader to transfer the trader's rights and obligations under the contract, where this may reduce the guarantees for the consumer, without the consumer's agreement.

20 A term which has the object or effect of excluding or hindering the consumer's right to take legal action or exercise any other legal remedy, in particular by—

(a) requiring the consumer to take disputes exclusively to arbitration not covered by legal provisions,

(b) unduly restricting the evidence available to the consumer, or

(c) imposing on the consumer a burden of proof which, according to the applicable law, should lie with another party to the contract.

PART 2

SCOPE OF PART 1

Financial services

21 Paragraph 8 (cancellation without reasonable notice) does not include a term by which a supplier of financial services reserves the right to terminate unilaterally a contract of indeterminate duration without notice where there is a valid reason, if the supplier is required to inform the consumer of the cancellation immediately.

22 Paragraph 11 (variation of contract without valid reason) does not include a term by which a supplier of financial services reserves the right to alter the rate of interest payable by or due to the consumer, or the amount of other charges for financial services without notice where there is a valid reason, if—

(a) the supplier is required to inform the consumer of the alteration at the earliest opportunity, and

(b) the consumer is free to dissolve the contract immediately.

Contracts which last indefinitely

23 Paragraphs 11 (variation of contract without valid reason), 12 (determination of characteristics of goods etc after consumer bound) and 14 (determination of price after consumer bound) do not include a term under which a trader reserves the right to alter unilaterally the conditions of a contract of indeterminate duration if—

(a) the trader is required to inform the consumer with reasonable notice, and

(b) the consumer is free to dissolve the contract.

Sale of securities, foreign currency etc

24 Paragraphs 8 (cancellation without reasonable notice), 11 (variation of contract without valid reason), 14 (determination of price after consumer bound) and 15 (increase in price) do not apply to—

(a) transactions in transferable securities, financial instruments and other products or services where the price is linked to fluctuations in a stock exchange quotation or index or a financial market rate that the trader does not control, and

(b) contracts for the purchase or sale of foreign currency, traveller's cheques or international money orders denominated in foreign currency.

Price index clauses

25 Paragraphs 14 (determination of price after consumer bound) and 15 (increase in price) do not include a term which is a price-indexation clause (where otherwise lawful), if the method by which prices vary is explicitly described.

SCHEDULE 3

Section 70

ENFORCEMENT OF THE LAW ON UNFAIR CONTRACT TERMS AND NOTICES

Application of Schedule

1 This Schedule applies to—

(a) a term of a consumer contract,

(b) a term proposed for use in a consumer contract,

(c) a term which a third party recommends for use in a consumer contract, or

(d) a consumer notice.

Consideration of complaints

2 (1) A regulator may consider a complaint about a term or notice to which this Schedule applies (a "relevant complaint").

(2) If a regulator other than the CMA intends to consider a relevant complaint, it must notify the CMA that it intends to do so, and must then consider the complaint.

(3) If a regulator considers a relevant complaint, but decides not to make an application under paragraph 3 in relation to the complaint, it must give reasons for its decision to the person who made the complaint.

Application for injunction or interdict

3 (1) A regulator may apply for an injunction or (in Scotland) an interdict against a person if the regulator thinks that—

(a) the person is using, or proposing or recommending the use of, a term or notice to which this Schedule applies, and

(b) the term or notice falls within any one or more of sub-paragraphs (2), (3) or (5).

(2) A term or notice falls within this sub-paragraph if it purports to exclude or restrict liability of the kind mentioned in—

(a) section 31 (exclusion of liability: goods contracts),

(b) section 47 (exclusion of liability: digital content contracts),

(c) section 57 (exclusion of liability: services contracts), or

(d) section 65(1) (business liability for death or personal injury resulting from negligence).

(3) A term or notice falls within this sub-paragraph if it is unfair to any extent.

(4) A term within paragraph 1(1)(b) or (c) (but not within paragraph 1(1)(a)) is to be treated for the purposes of section 62(4) and (5) (assessment of fairness) as if it were a term of a contract.

(5) A term or notice falls within this sub-paragraph if it breaches section 68 (requirement for transparency).

(6) A regulator may apply for an injunction or interdict under this paragraph in relation to a term or notice whether or not it has received a relevant complaint about the term or notice.

Notification of application

4 (1) Before making an application under paragraph 3, a regulator other than the CMA must notify the CMA that it intends to do so.

(2) The regulator may make the application only if—

(a) the period of 14 days beginning with the day on which the regulator notified the CMA has ended, or

(b) before the end of that period, the CMA agrees to the regulator making the application.

Determination of application

5 (1) On an application for an injunction under paragraph 3, the court may grant an injunction on such conditions, and against such of the respondents, as it thinks appropriate.

(2) On an application for an interdict under paragraph 3, the court may grant an interdict on such conditions, and against such of the defenders, as it thinks appropriate.

(3) The injunction or interdict may include provision about—

(a) a term or notice to which the application relates, or

(b) any term of a consumer contract, or any consumer notice, of a similar kind or with a similar effect.

(4) It is not a defence to an application under paragraph 3 to show that, because of a rule of law, a term to which the application relates is not, or could not be, an enforceable contract term.

(5) If a regulator other than the CMA makes the application, it must notify the CMA of—

(a) the outcome of the application, and

(b) if an injunction or interdict is granted, the conditions on which, and the persons against whom, it is granted.

Undertakings

6 (1) A regulator may accept an undertaking from a person against whom it has applied, or thinks it is entitled to apply, for an injunction or interdict under paragraph 3.

(2) The undertaking may provide that the person will comply with the conditions that are agreed between the person and the regulator about the use of terms or notices, or terms or notices of a kind, specified in the undertaking.

(3) If a regulator other than the CMA accepts an undertaking, it must notify the CMA of—

(a) the conditions on which the undertaking is accepted, and

(b) the person who gave it.

Publication, information and advice

7 (1) The CMA must arrange the publication of details of—

(a) any application it makes for an injunction or interdict under paragraph 3,

(b) any injunction or interdict under this Schedule, and

(c) any undertaking under this Schedule.

(2) The CMA must respond to a request whether a term or notice, or one of a similar kind or with a similar effect, is or has been the subject of an injunction, interdict or undertaking under this Schedule.

(3) Where the term or notice, or one of a similar kind or with a similar effect, is or has been the subject of an injunction or interdict under this Schedule, the CMA must give the person making the request a copy of the injunction or interdict.

(4) Where the term or notice, or one of a similar kind or with a similar effect, is or has been the subject of an undertaking under this Schedule, the CMA must give the person making the request—

(a) details of the undertaking, and

(b) if the person giving the undertaking has agreed to amend the term or notice, a copy of the amendments.

(5) The CMA may arrange the publication of advice and information about the provisions of this Part.

(6) In this paragraph—

(a) references to an injunction or interdict under this Schedule are to an injunction or interdict granted on an application by the CMA under paragraph 3 or notified to it under paragraph 5, and

(b) references to an undertaking are to an undertaking given to the CMA under paragraph 6 or notified to it under that paragraph.

Meaning of "regulator"

8 (1) In this Schedule "regulator" means—

(a) the CMA,

(b) the Department of Enterprise, Trade and Investment in Northern Ireland,
(c) a local weights and measures authority in Great Britain,
(d) the Financial Conduct Authority,
(e) the Office of Communications,
(f) the Information Commissioner,
(g) the Gas and Electricity Markets Authority,
(h) the Water Services Regulation Authority,
(i) the Office of Rail Regulation,
(j) the Northern Ireland Authority for Utility Regulation, or
(k) the Consumers' Association.

(2) The Secretary of State may by order made by statutory instrument amend sub-paragraph (1) so as to add, modify or remove an entry.

(3) An order under sub-paragraph (2) may amend sub-paragraph (1) so as to add a body that is not a public authority only if the Secretary of State thinks that the body represents the interests of consumers (or consumers of a particular description).

(4) The Secretary of State must publish (and may from time to time vary) other criteria to be applied by the Secretary of State in deciding whether to add an entry to, or remove an entry from, sub-paragraph (1).

(5) An order under sub-paragraph (2) may make consequential amendments to this Schedule (including with the effect that any of its provisions apply differently, or do not apply, to a body added to sub-paragraph (1)).

(6) An order under sub-paragraph (2) may contain transitional or transitory provision or savings.

(7) No order may be made under sub-paragraph (2) unless a draft of the statutory instrument containing it has been laid before, and approved by a resolution of, each House of Parliament.

(8) In this paragraph "public authority" has the same meaning as in section 6 of the Human Rights Act 1998.

Other definitions

9 In this Schedule—

"the CMA" means the Competition and Markets Authority;
"injunction" includes an interim injunction;
"interdict" includes an interim interdict.

The Financial Conduct Authority

10 The functions of the Financial Conduct Authority under this Schedule are to be treated as functions of the Authority under the Financial Services and Markets Act 2000.

SCHEDULE 4

Section 75

AMENDMENTS CONSEQUENTIAL ON PART 2

Misrepresentation Act 1967 (c. 7)

1 (1) Section 3 of the Misrepresentation Act 1967 (avoidance of provision excluding liability for misrepresentation) is amended as follows.

(2) At the beginning insert "(1)".

(3) At the end insert—

"(2) This section does not apply to a term in a consumer contract within the meaning of Part 2 of the Consumer Rights Act 2015 (but see the provision made about such contracts in section 62 of that Act)."

Unfair Contract Terms Act 1977 (c. 50)

2 The Unfair Contract Terms Act 1977 is amended as follows.

3 In section 1(2) (scope of Part 1) for "to 4" substitute ", 3".

4 In section 2 (negligence liability), after subsection (3) insert—

"(4) This section does not apply to—

(a) a term in a consumer contract, or

(b) a notice to the extent that it is a consumer notice,

(but see the provision made about such contracts and notices in sections 62 and 65 of the Consumer Rights Act 2015)."

5 (1) Section 3 (liability arising in contract) is amended as follows.

(2) In subsection (1) omit "as consumer or".

(3) After subsection (2) insert—

"(3) This section does not apply to a term in a consumer contract (but see the provision made about such contracts in section 62 of the Consumer Rights Act 2015)."

6 Omit section 4 (unreasonable indemnity clauses).

7 Omit section 5 ("guarantee" of consumer goods).

8 (1) Section 6 (sale and hire-purchase) is amended as follows.

(2) After subsection (1) insert—

"(1A) Liability for breach of the obligations arising from—

(a) section 13, 14 or 15 of the 1979 Act (seller's implied undertakings as to conformity of goods with description or sample, or as to their quality or fitness for a particular purpose);

(b) section 9, 10 or 11 of the 1973 Act (the corresponding things in relation to hire purchase),

cannot be excluded or restricted by reference to a contract term except in so far as the term satisfies the requirement of reasonableness."

(3) Omit subsections (2) and (3).

(4) After subsection (4) insert—

"(5) This section does not apply to a consumer contract (but see the provision made about such contracts in section 31 of the Consumer Rights Act 2015)."

9 (1) Section 7 (miscellaneous contracts under which goods pass) is amended as follows.

(2) After subsection (1) insert—

"(1A) Liability in respect of the goods' correspondence with description or sample, or their quality or fitness for any particular purpose, cannot be excluded or restricted by reference to such a term except in so far as the term satisfies the requirement of reasonableness."

(3) Omit subsections (2) and (3).

(4) After subsection (4) insert—

"(4A) This section does not apply to a consumer contract (but see the provision made about such contracts in section 31 of the Consumer Rights Act 2015)."

10 Omit section 9 (effect of breach of contract).

11 Omit section 12 ("dealing as consumer").

12 In section 13(1) (varieties of exemption clauses) for "and 5 to" substitute ", 6 and".

13 In section 14 (interpretation of Part 1), at the appropriate places insert—

""consumer contract" has the same meaning as in the Consumer Rights Act 2015 (see section 61);";

""consumer notice" has the same meaning as in the Consumer Rights Act 2015 (see section 61);".

14 (1) Section 15 (scope of Part 2) is amended as follows.

(2) In subsection (2) for "to 18" substitute "and 17".

(3) In subsection (3)—

(a) for "to 18" substitute "and 17", and

(b) in paragraph (b) omit sub-paragraph (ii) and the "or" preceding it.

15 In section 16 (liability for breach of duty), after subsection (3) insert—

"(4) This section does not apply to—

(a) a term in a consumer contract, or

(b) a notice to the extent that it is a consumer notice,

(but see the provision made about such contracts and notices in sections 62 and 65 of the Consumer Rights Act 2015)."

16 (1) Section 17 (control of unreasonable exemptions in consumer or standard form contracts) is amended as follows.

(2) In the heading omit "consumer or".

(3) In subsection (1)—

(a) omit "a consumer contract or",

(b) in paragraph (a) omit "consumer or", and

(c) in paragraph (b) omit "consumer or".

(4) After subsection (2) insert—

"(3) This section does not apply to a term in a consumer contract (but see the provision made about such contracts in section 62 of the Consumer Rights Act 2015)."

17 Omit section 18 (unreasonable indemnity clauses in consumer contracts).

18 Omit section 19 ("guarantee" of consumer goods).

19 (1) Section 20 (obligations implied by law in sale and hire-purchase contracts) is amended as follows.

(2) After subsection (1) insert—

"(1A) Any term of a contract which purports to exclude or restrict liability for breach of the obligations arising from—

(a) section 13, 14 or 15 of the 1979 Act (seller's implied undertakings as to conformity of goods with description or sample, or as to their quality or fitness for a particular purpose);

(b) section 9, 10 or 11 of the 1973 Act (the corresponding things in relation to hire purchase),

shall have effect only if it was fair and reasonable to incorporate the term in the contract.

(1B) This section does not apply to a consumer contract (but see the provision made about such contracts in section 31 of the Consumer Rights Act 2015)."

(3) Omit subsection (2).

20 (1) Section 21 (obligations implied by law in other contracts for the supply of goods) is amended as follows.

(2) In subsection (1), for paragraphs (a) and (b) substitute "such as is referred to in subsection (3) below shall have no effect if it was not fair and reasonable to incorporate the term in the contract."

(3) In subsection (2)(b) omit "unless it is a consumer contract (and then only in favour of the consumer)".

(4) After subsection (3A) insert—

"(3B) This section does not apply to a consumer contract (but see the provision made about such contracts in section 31 of the Consumer Rights Act 2015)."

21 Omit section 22 (consequence of breach of contract).

22 (1) Section 25 (interpretation of Part 2) is amended as follows.

(2) In subsection (1)—

(a) omit the definition of "consumer",

(b) for the definition of "consumer contract" substitute—

""consumer contract" has the same meaning as in the Consumer Rights Act 2015 (see section 61);", and

(c) at the appropriate place insert—

"""consumer notice" has the same meaning as in the Consumer Rights Act 2015 (see section 61);".

(3) Omit subsections (1A) and (1B).

(4) In subsection (5), for "and 16 and 19 to" substitute ", 16, 20 and".

23 In section 26(2) (international supply contracts) omit "or 4".

24 (1) Section 27 (choice of law clauses) is amended as follows.

(2) In subsection (2)—

(a) omit "(either or both)", and

(b) omit paragraph (b) and the "or" preceding it.

(3) Omit subsection (3).

25 Omit section 28 (temporary provision for sea carriage of passengers).

26 (1) Schedule 1 (scope of sections 2 to 4 and 7) is amended as follows.

(2) In the heading, for "to 4" substitute ", 3".

(3) In paragraph 1, for "to 4" substitute "and 3".

(4) In paragraph 2—

(a) for "to 4" substitute ", 3", and

(b) omit "except in favour of a person dealing as consumer".

(5) In paragraph 3—

(a) for ", 3 and 4" substitute "and 3", and

(b) omit ", except in favour of a person dealing as consumer,".

27 In Schedule 2 ("guidelines" for application of reasonableness test), for "6(3), 7(3) and (4)," substitute "6(1A), 7(1A) and (4),".

Companies Act 1985 (c. 6)

28 (1) Schedule 15D to the Companies Act 1985 (specified descriptions of disclosures for the purposes of section 449) is amended as follows.

(2) In paragraph 17—

(a) omit paragraph (i), and

(b) after paragraph (l) insert—

"(m) Schedule 3 to the Consumer Rights Act 2015".

(3) For paragraph 25 substitute—

"25 A disclosure for the purposes of enabling or assisting a regulator under Schedule 3 to the Consumer Rights Act 2015 other than the Competition and Markets Authority to exercise its functions under that Schedule."

Merchant Shipping Act 1995 (c. 21)

29 In section 184 of the Merchant Shipping Act 1995 (application of Schedule 6 to carriage within British Islands) omit subsection (2).

Arbitration Act 1996 (c. 23)

30 The Arbitration Act 1996 is amended as follows.

31 (1) Section 89 (application of unfair terms regulations to consumer arbitration agreements) is amended as follows.

(2) In subsection (1), for "the Unfair Terms in Consumer Contracts Regulations 1994" substitute "Part 2 (unfair terms) of the Consumer Rights Act 2015".

(3) For subsection (2) substitute—

> "(2) In those sections "the Part" means Part 2 (unfair terms) of the Consumer Rights Act 2015."

32 For section 90 (regulations apply where consumer is a legal person) substitute—

"90 Part applies where consumer is a legal person

"90 Part applies where consumer is a legal person

> The Part applies where the consumer is a legal person as it applies where the consumer is an individual."

33 In section 91(1) (arbitration agreement unfair where modest amount sought) for "Regulations" substitute "Part".

Unfair Terms in Consumer Contracts Regulations 1999 (S.I. 1999/2083)

34 The Unfair Terms in Consumer Contracts Regulations 1999 are revoked.

Enterprise Act 2002 (c. 40)

35 In Schedule 15 to the Enterprise Act 2002 (enactments for the purposes of which disclosures may be made), at the end insert—

> "Schedule 3 to the Consumer Rights Act 2015."

Companies Act 2006 (c. 46)

36 The Companies Act 2006 is amended as follows.

37 (1) Section (A) of Part 2 of Schedule 2 (specified descriptions of disclosures for the purposes of section 948) is amended as follows.

(2) In paragraph 25—

(a) omit paragraph (h), and

(b) after paragraph (k) insert—

> "(l) Schedule 3 to the Consumer Rights Act 2015".

(3) For paragraph 33 substitute—

> "33 A disclosure for the purposes of enabling or assisting a regulator under Schedule 3 to the Consumer Rights Act 2015 other than the Competition and Markets Authority to exercise its functions under that Schedule."

38 (1) Part 2 of Schedule 11A (specified descriptions of disclosures for the purposes of section 1224A) is amended as follows.

(2) In paragraph 39, for paragraph (i) insert—

"(i) Schedule 3 to the Consumer Rights Act 2015".

(3) For paragraph 48 substitute—

"48 A disclosure for the purposes of enabling or assisting a regulator under Schedule 3 to the Consumer Rights Act 2015 other than the Competition and Markets Authority to exercise its functions under that Schedule."

Consequential repeals

39 In consequence of the amendments made by this Schedule—

(a) omit paragraph 19(b) of Schedule 2 to the Sale of Goods Act 1979, and

(b) in paragraph 21 of that Schedule, omit "and (2)(a)" and "(in each case)".

SCHEDULE 5

Section 77

INVESTIGATORY POWERS ETC.

PART 1

BASIC CONCEPTS

Overview

1 (1) This Schedule confers investigatory powers on enforcers and specifies the purposes for which and the circumstances in which those powers may be exercised.

(2) Part 1 of this Schedule contains interpretation provisions; in particular paragraphs 2 to 6 explain what is meant by an "enforcer".

(3) Part 2 of this Schedule explains what is meant by "the enforcer's legislation".

(4) Part 3 of this Schedule contains powers in relation to the production of information; paragraph 13 sets out which enforcers may exercise those powers, and the purposes for which they may do so.

(5) Part 4 of this Schedule contains further powers; paragraphs 19 and 20 set out which enforcers may exercise those powers, and the purposes for which they may do so.

(6) Part 5 of this Schedule contains provisions that are supplementary to the powers in Parts 3 and 4 of this Schedule.

(7) Part 6 of this Schedule makes provision about the exercise of functions by certain enforcers outside their area or district and the bringing of proceedings in relation to conduct outside an enforcer's area or district.

Enforcers

2 (1) In this Schedule "enforcer" means—

(a) a domestic enforcer,

(b) an EU enforcer,
(c) a public designated enforcer, or
(d) an unfair contract terms enforcer.

(2) But in Part 4 and paragraphs 38 and 41 of this Schedule "enforcer" means—
(a) a domestic enforcer, or
(b) an EU enforcer.

(3) In paragraphs 13, 19 and 20 of this Schedule, a reference to an enforcer exercising a power includes a reference to an officer of the enforcer exercising that power.

Domestic enforcers

3 (1) In this Schedule "domestic enforcer" means—
(a) the Competition and Markets Authority,
(b) a local weights and measures authority in Great Britain,
(c) a district council in England,
(d) the Department of Enterprise, Trade and Investment in Northern Ireland,
(e) a district council in Northern Ireland,
(f) the Secretary of State,
(g) the Gas and Electricity Markets Authority,
(h) the British Hallmarking Council,
(i) an assay office within the meaning of the Hallmarking Act 1973, or
(j) any other person to whom the duty in subsection (1) of section 27 of the Consumer Protection Act 1987 (duty to enforce safety provisions) applies by virtue of regulations under subsection (2) of that section.

(2) But the Gas and Electricity Markets Authority is not a domestic enforcer for the purposes of Part 4 of this Schedule.

(3) The reference to the Department of Enterprise, Trade and Investment in Northern Ireland includes a person with whom the Department has made arrangements, under paragraph 3(1) of Schedule 15 to the Lifts Regulations 1997 (SI 1997/831) for enforcement of those regulations.

EU enforcers

4 In this Schedule "EU enforcer" means—
(a) the Competition and Markets Authority,
(b) a local weights and measures authority in Great Britain,
(c) the Department of Enterprise, Trade and Investment in Northern Ireland,
(d) the Financial Conduct Authority,
(e) the Civil Aviation Authority,
(f) the Secretary of State,
(g) the Department of Health, Social Services and Public Safety in Northern Ireland,
(h) the Office of Communications,
(i) an enforcement authority within the meaning of section 120(15) of the Communications Act 2003 (regulation of premium rate services), or
(j) the Information Commissioner.

Public designated enforcers

5 In this Schedule "public designated enforcer" means a person or body which—

(a) is designated by order under subsection (2) of section 213 of the Enterprise Act 2002, and

(b) has been designated by virtue of subsection (3) of that section (which provides that the Secretary of State may designate a public body only if satisfied that it is independent).

Unfair contract terms enforcer

6 In this Schedule "unfair contract terms enforcer" means a person or body which—

(a) is for the time being listed in paragraph 8(1) of Schedule 3 (persons or bodies that may enforce provisions about unfair contract terms), and

(b) is a public authority within the meaning of section 6 of the Human Rights Act 1998.

Officers

7 (1) In this Schedule "officer", in relation to an enforcer, means—

(a) an inspector appointed by the enforcer to exercise powers under this Schedule, or authorised to do so,

(b) an officer of the enforcer appointed by the enforcer to exercise powers under this Schedule, or authorised to do so,

(c) an employee of the enforcer (other than an inspector or officer) appointed by the enforcer to exercise powers under this Schedule, or authorised to do so, or

(d) a person (other than an inspector, officer or employee of the enforcer) authorised by the enforcer to exercise powers under this Schedule.

(2) But references in this Schedule to an officer in relation to a particular power only cover a person within sub-paragraph (1) if and to the extent that the person has been appointed or authorised to exercise that power.

(3) A person who, immediately before the coming into force of this Schedule, was appointed or authorised to exercise a power replaced by a power in this Schedule is to be treated as having been appointed or authorised to exercise the new power.

(4) In this paragraph "employee", in relation to the Secretary of State, means a person employed in the civil service of the State.

Interpretation of other terms

8 In this Schedule—

"Community infringement" has the same meaning as in section 212 of the Enterprise Act 2002;

"document" includes information recorded in any form;

"enforcement order" means an order under section 217 of the Enterprise Act 2002;

"interim enforcement order" means an order under section 218 of that Act;

"the Regulation on Accreditation and Market Surveillance" means Regulation (EC) No 765/2008 of the European Parliament and of the Council of 9 July 2008 setting out the requirements for accreditation and market surveillance relating to the marketing of products and repealing Regulation (EEC) No 339/93.

PART 2

THE ENFORCER'S LEGISLATION

Enforcer's legislation

9 (1) In this Schedule "the enforcer's legislation", in relation to a domestic enforcer, means—

(a) legislation or notices which, by virtue of a provision listed in paragraph 10, the domestic enforcer has a duty or power to enforce, and

(b) where the domestic enforcer is listed in an entry in the first column of the table in paragraph 11, the legislation listed in the corresponding entry in the second column of that table.

(2) References in this Schedule to a breach of or compliance with the enforcer's legislation include a breach of or compliance with a notice issued under—

(a) the enforcer's legislation, or

(b) legislation under which the enforcer's legislation is made.

(3) References in this Schedule to a breach of or compliance with the enforcer's legislation are to be read, in relation to the Lifts Regulations 1997 (SI 1997/831), as references to a breach of or compliance with the Regulations as they apply to relevant products (within the meaning of Schedule 15 to the Regulations) for private use or consumption.

Enforcer's legislation: duties and powers mentioned in paragraph 9(1)(a)

10 The duties and powers mentioned in paragraph 9(1)(a) are those arising under any of the following provisions—

"section 26(1) or 40(1)(b) of the Trade Descriptions Act 1968 (including as applied by regulation 8(3) of the Crystal Glass (Descriptions) Regulations 1973 (SI 1973/1952) and regulation 10(2) of the Footwear (Indication of Composition) Labelling Regulations 1995 (SI 1995/2489));

section 9(1) or (6) of the Hallmarking Act 1973;

paragraph 6 of the Schedule to the Prices Act 1974 (including as read with paragraph 14(1) of that Schedule);

section 161(1) of the Consumer Credit Act 1974;

section 26(1) of the Estate Agents Act 1979;

Article 39 of the Weights and Measures (Northern Ireland) Order 1981 (SI 1981/231 (NI 10));

section 16A(1) or (4) of the Video Recordings Act 1984;

section 27(1) of the Consumer Protection Act 1987 (including as applied by section 12(1) of the Fireworks Act 2003 to fireworks regulations under that Act);

section 215(1) of the Education Reform Act 1988;

section 107A(1) or (3) or 198A(1) or (3) of the Copyright, Designs and Patents Act 1988;

paragraph 3(a) of Schedule 5 to the Simple Pressure Vessels (Safety) Regulations 1991 (SI 1991/2749);

paragraph 1 of Schedule 3 to the Package Travel, Package Holidays and Package Tours Regulations 1992 (SI 1992/3288);

section 30(4) or (7) or 31(4)(a) of the Clean Air Act 1993;

paragraph 1 of Schedule 2 to the Sunday Trading Act 1994;

section 93(1) or (3) of the Trade Marks Act 1994;

section 8A(1) or (3) of the Olympic Symbol etc (Protection) Act 1995;

paragraph 2(a) or 3(1) of Schedule 15 to the Lifts Regulations 1997 (SI 1997/831);

paragraph 2(a) or 3(3)(a) of Schedule 8 to the Pressure Equipment Regulations 1999 (SI 1999/2001);

regulation 5C(5) of the Motor Fuel (Composition and Content) Regulations 1999 (SI 1999/3107);

paragraph 1(1)(b) or (2)(b) or 2 of Schedule 9 to the Radio Equipment and Telecommunications Terminal Equipment Regulations 2000 (SI 2000/730);

paragraph 1(a) of Schedule 10 to the Personal Protective Equipment Regulations 2002 (SI 2002/1144);

paragraph 1 of Schedule 4 to the Packaging (Essential Requirements) Regulations 2003 (SI 2003/1941);

section 3(1) of the Christmas Day Trading Act 2004;

regulation 10(1) of the General Product Safety Regulations 2005 (SI 2005/1803);

regulation 10(1) of the Weights and Measures (Packaged Goods) Regulations 2006 (SI 2006/659);

regulation 17 of the Measuring Instruments (Automatic Discontinuous Totalisers) Regulations 2006 (SI 2006/1255);

regulation 18 of the Measuring Instruments (Automatic Rail-weighbridges) Regulations 2006 (SI 2006/1256);

regulation 20 of the Measuring Instruments (Automatic Catchweighers) Regulations 2006 (SI 2006/1257);

regulation 18 of the Measuring Instruments (Automatic Gravimetric Filling Instruments) Regulations 2006 (SI 2006/1258);

regulation 18 of the Measuring Instruments (Beltweighers) Regulations 2006 (SI 2006/1259);

regulation 16 of the Measuring Instruments (Capacity Serving Measures) Regulations 2006 (SI 2006/1264);

regulation 17 of the Measuring Instruments (Liquid Fuel and Lubricants) Regulations 2006 (SI 2006/1266);

regulation 16 of the Measuring Instruments (Material Measures of Length) Regulations 2006 (SI 2006/1267);

regulation 17 of the Measuring Instruments (Cold-water Meters) Regulations 2006 (SI 2006/1268);

regulation 18 of the Measuring Instruments (Liquid Fuel delivered from Road Tankers) Regulations 2006 (SI 2006/1269);

regulation 37(1)(a)(ii) or (b)(ii) of the Electromagnetic Compatibility Regulations 2006 (SI 2006/3418);

regulation 13(1) or (1A) of the Business Protection from Misleading Marketing Regulations 2008 (SI 2008/1276);

regulation 19(1) or (1A) of the Consumer Protection from Unfair Trading Regulations 2008 (SI 2008/1277);

paragraph 2 or 5 of Schedule 5 to the Supply of Machinery (Safety) Regulations 2008 (SI 2008/1597);

regulation 32(2) or (3) of the Timeshare, Holiday Products, Resale and Exchange Contracts Regulations 2010 (SI 2010/2960);

regulation 10(1) of the Weights and Measures (Packaged Goods) Regulations (Northern Ireland) 2011 (SR 2011/331);

regulation 11 of the Textile Products (Labelling and Fibre Composition) Regulations 2012 (SI 2012/1102);

regulation 6(1) of the Cosmetic Products Enforcement Regulations 2013 (SI 2013/1478);

section 87(1) of this Act;

section 93(1) or (2) of this Act."

Enforcer's legislation: legislation mentioned in paragraph 9(1)(b)

11 Here is the table mentioned in paragraph 9(1)(b)—

Enforcer	*Legislation*
A local weights and measures authority in Great Britain or the Department of Enterprise, Trade and Investment in Northern Ireland	Section 35ZA of the Registered Designs Act 1949
A local weights and measures authority in Great Britain or the Department of Enterprise, Trade and Investment in Northern Ireland	The Measuring Container Bottles (EEC Requirements) Regulations 1977 (SI 1977/932)
The Secretary of State	The Alcoholometers and Alcohol Hydrometers (EEC Requirements) Regulations 1977 (SI 1977/1753)
A local weights and measures authority in Great Britain	The Weights and Measures Act 1985 and regulations and orders made under that Act
A local weights and measures authority in Great Britain or the Department of Enterprise, Trade and Investment in Northern Ireland	The Measuring Instruments (EEC Requirements) Regulations 1988 (SI 1988/186)
A local weights and measures authority in Great Britain or the Department of Enterprise, Trade and Investment in Northern Ireland	The Financial Services and Markets Act 2000 so far as it relates to a relevant regulated activity within the meaning of section 107(4)(a) of the Financial Services Act 2012

Enforcer	*Legislation*
A local weights and measures authority in Great Britain or the Department of Enterprise, Trade and Investment in Northern Ireland	The Non-Automatic Weighing Instruments Regulations 2000 (SI 2000/3236)

Powers to amend paragraph 10 or 11

12 (1) The Secretary of State may by order made by statutory instrument—

(a) amend paragraph 10 or the table in paragraph 11 by adding, modifying or removing any entry in it;

(b) in consequence of provision made under paragraph (a), amend, repeal or revoke any other legislation (including this Act) whenever passed or made.

(2) The Secretary of State may not make an order under this paragraph that has the effect that a power of entry, or an associated power, contained in legislation other than this Act is replaced by a power of entry, or an associated power, contained in this Schedule unless the Secretary of State thinks that the condition in sub-paragraph (3) is met.

(3) That condition is that, on and after the changes made by the order, the safeguards applicable to the new power, taken together, provide a greater level of protection than any safeguards applicable to the old power.

(4) In sub-paragraph (2) "power of entry" and "associated power" have the meanings given by section 46 of the Protection of Freedoms Act 2012.

(5) An order under this paragraph may contain transitional or transitory provision or savings.

(6) A statutory instrument containing an order under this paragraph that amends or repeals primary legislation may not be made unless a draft of the instrument containing the order has been laid before, and approved by a resolution of, each House of Parliament.

(7) Any other statutory instrument containing an order under this paragraph is subject to annulment in pursuance of a resolution of either House of Parliament.

(8) In this paragraph "primary legislation" means—

(a) an Act of Parliament,

(b) an Act of the Scottish Parliament,

(c) an Act or Measure of the National Assembly for Wales, or

(d) Northern Ireland legislation.

PART 3

POWERS IN RELATION TO THE PRODUCTION OF INFORMATION

Exercise of powers in this Part

13 (1) An enforcer of a kind mentioned in this paragraph may exercise a power in this Part of this Schedule only for the purposes and in the circumstances mentioned in this paragraph in relation to that kind of enforcer.

(2) The Competition and Markets Authority may exercise the powers in this Part of this Schedule for any of the following purposes—

(a) to enable the Authority to exercise or to consider whether to exercise any function it has under Part 8 of the Enterprise Act 2002;

(b) to enable a private designated enforcer to consider whether to exercise any function it has under that Part;

(c) to enable a Community enforcer to consider whether to exercise any function it has under that Part;

(d) to ascertain whether a person has complied with or is complying with an enforcement order or an interim enforcement order;

(e) to ascertain whether a person has complied with or is complying with an undertaking given under section 217(9), 218(10) or 219 of the Enterprise Act 2002.

(3) A public designated enforcer, a local weights and measures authority in Great Britain, the Department of Enterprise, Trade and Investment in Northern Ireland or an EU enforcer other than the Competition and Markets Authority may exercise the powers in this Part of this Schedule for any of the following purposes—

(a) to enable that enforcer to exercise or to consider whether to exercise any function it has under Part 8 of the Enterprise Act 2002;

(b) to ascertain whether a person has complied with or is complying with an enforcement order or an interim enforcement order made on the application of that enforcer;

(c) to ascertain whether a person has complied with or is complying with an undertaking given under section 217(9) or 218(10) of the Enterprise Act 2002 following such an application;

(d) to ascertain whether a person has complied with or is complying with an undertaking given to that enforcer under section 219 of that Act.

(4) A domestic enforcer may exercise the powers in this Part of this Schedule for the purpose of ascertaining whether there has been a breach of the enforcer's legislation.

(5) But a domestic enforcer may not exercise the power in paragraph 14 (power to require the production of information) for the purpose in sub-paragraph (4) unless an officer of the enforcer reasonably suspects a breach of the enforcer's legislation.

(6) Sub-paragraph (5) does not apply if the enforcer is a market surveillance authority within the meaning of Article 2(18) of the Regulation on Accreditation and Market Surveillance and the power is exercised for the purpose of market surveillance within the meaning of Article 2(17) of that Regulation.

(7) An unfair contract terms enforcer may exercise the powers in this Part of this Schedule for either of the following purposes—

(a) to enable the enforcer to exercise or to consider whether to exercise any function it has under Schedule 3 (enforcement of the law on unfair contract terms and notices);

(b) to ascertain whether a person has complied with or is complying with an injunction or interdict (within the meaning of that Schedule) granted under paragraph 5 of that Schedule or an undertaking given under paragraph 6 of that Schedule.

(8) But an unfair contract terms enforcer may not exercise the power in paragraph 14 for a purpose mentioned in sub-paragraph (7)(a) unless an officer of the enforcer reasonably suspects that a person is using, or proposing or recommending the use of, a contractual term or notice within paragraph 3 of Schedule 3.

(9) A local weights and measures authority in Great Britain may exercise the powers in this Part of this Schedule for either of the following purposes—

(a) to enable it to determine whether to make an order under section 3 or 4 of the Estate Agents Act 1979;

(b) to enable it to exercise any of its functions under section 5, 6, 8, 13 or 17 of that Act.

(10) In this paragraph—

"Community enforcer" has the same meaning as in the Enterprise Act 2002 (see section 213(5) of that Act);

"private designated enforcer" means a person or body which—

(a) is designated by order under subsection (2) of section 213 of that Act, and

(b) has been designated by virtue of subsection (4) of that section (which provides that the Secretary of State may designate a person or body which is not a public body only if it satisfies criteria specified by order).

Power to require the production of information

14 An enforcer or an officer of an enforcer may give notice to a person requiring the person to provide the enforcer with the information specified in the notice.

Procedure for notice under paragraph 14

15 (1) A notice under paragraph 14 must be in writing and specify the purpose for which the information is required.

(2) If the purpose is to enable a person to exercise or to consider whether to exercise a function, the notice must specify the function concerned.

(3) The notice may specify—

(a) the time within which and the manner in which the person to whom it is given must comply with it;

(b) the form in which information must be provided.

(4) The notice may require—

(a) the creation of documents, or documents of a description, specified in the notice, and

(b) the provision of those documents to the enforcer or an officer of the enforcer.

(5) A requirement to provide information or create a document is a requirement to do so in a legible form.

(6) A notice under paragraph 14 does not require a person to provide any information or create any documents which the person would be entitled to refuse to provide or produce—

(a) in proceedings in the High Court on the grounds of legal professional privilege, or

(b) in proceedings in the Court of Session on the grounds of confidentiality of communications.

(7) In sub-paragraph (6) "communications" means—

(a) communications between a professional legal adviser and the adviser's client, or

(b) communications made in connection with or in contemplation of legal proceedings or for the purposes of those proceedings.

Enforcement of notice under paragraph 14

16 (1) If a person fails to comply with a notice under paragraph 14, the enforcer or an officer of the enforcer may make an application under this paragraph to the court.

(2) If it appears to the court that the person has failed to comply with the notice, it may make an order under this paragraph.

(3) An order under this paragraph is an order requiring the person to do anything that the court thinks it is reasonable for the person to do, for any of the purposes for which the notice was given, to ensure that the notice is complied with.

(4) An order under this paragraph may require the person to meet the costs or expenses of the application.

(5) If the person is a company, partnership or unincorporated association, the court in acting under sub-paragraph (4) may require an official who is responsible for the failure to meet the costs or expenses.

(6) In this paragraph—

"the court" means—

(a) the High Court,

(b) in relation to England and Wales, the county court,

(c) in relation to Northern Ireland, a county court,

(d) the Court of Session, or

(e) the sheriff;

"official" means—

(a) in the case of a company, a director, manager, secretary or other similar officer,

(b) in the case of a limited liability partnership, a member,

(c) in the case of a partnership other than a limited liability partnership, a partner, and

(d) in the case of an unincorporated association, a person who is concerned in the management or control of its affairs.

Limitations on use of information provided in response to a notice under paragraph 14

17 (1) This paragraph applies if a person provides information in response to a notice under paragraph 14.

(2) This includes information contained in a document created by a person in response to such a notice.

(3) In any criminal proceedings against the person—

(a) no evidence relating to the information may be adduced by or on behalf of the prosecution, and

(b) no question relating to the information may be asked by or on behalf of the prosecution.

(4) Sub-paragraph (3) does not apply if, in the proceedings—

(a) evidence relating to the information is adduced by or on behalf of the person providing it, or

(b) a question relating to the information is asked by or on behalf of that person.

(5) Sub-paragraph (3) does not apply if the proceedings are for—

(a) an offence under paragraph 36 (obstruction),

(b) an offence under section 5 of the Perjury Act 1911 (false statutory declarations and other false statements without oath),

(c) an offence under section 44(2) of the Criminal Law (Consolidation) (Scotland) Act 1995 (false statements and declarations), or

(d) an offence under Article 10 of the Perjury (Northern Ireland) Order 1979 (SI 1979/1714 (NI 19)) (false statutory declarations and other false unsworn statements).

Application to Crown

18 In its application in relation to—

(a) an enforcer acting for a purpose within paragraph 13(2) or (3), or

(b) an enforcer acting for the purpose of ascertaining whether there has been a breach of the Consumer Protection from Unfair Trading Regulations 2008 (SI 2008/1277),

this Part binds the Crown.

PART 4

FURTHER POWERS EXERCISABLE BY DOMESTIC ENFORCERS AND EU ENFORCERS

Exercise of powers in this Part: domestic enforcers

19 (1) A domestic enforcer may exercise a power in this Part of this Schedule only for the purposes and in the circumstances mentioned in this paragraph in relation to that power.

(2) A domestic enforcer may exercise any power in paragraphs 21 to 26 and 31 to 34 for the purpose of ascertaining compliance with the enforcer's legislation.

(3) A domestic enforcer may exercise the power in paragraph 27 (power to require the production of documents) for either of the following purposes—

(a) subject to sub-paragraph (4), to ascertain compliance with the enforcer's legislation;

(b) to ascertain whether the documents may be required as evidence in proceedings for a breach of, or under, the enforcer's legislation.

(4) A domestic enforcer may exercise the power in paragraph 27 for the purpose mentioned in sub-paragraph (3)(a) only if an officer of the enforcer reasonably suspects a breach of the enforcer's legislation, unless—

(a) the power is being exercised in relation to a document that the trader is required to keep by virtue of a provision of the enforcer's legislation, or

(b) the enforcer is a market surveillance authority within the meaning of Article 2(18) of the Regulation on Accreditation and Market Surveillance and the power is exercised for the purpose of market surveillance within the meaning of Article 2(17) of that Regulation.

(5) A domestic enforcer may exercise the power in paragraph 28 (power to seize and detain goods) in relation to—

(a) goods which an officer of the enforcer reasonably suspects may disclose (by means of testing or otherwise) a breach of the enforcer's legislation,

(b) goods which an officer of the enforcer reasonably suspects are liable to forfeiture under that legislation, and

(c) goods which an officer of the enforcer reasonably suspects may be required as evidence in proceedings for a breach of, or under, that legislation.

(6) A domestic enforcer may exercise the power in paragraph 29 (power to seize documents required as evidence) in relation to documents which an officer of the enforcer reasonably suspects may be required as evidence—

(a) in proceedings for a breach of the enforcer's legislation, or

(b) in proceedings under the enforcer's legislation.

(7) A domestic enforcer may exercise the power in paragraph 30 (power to decommission or switch off fixed installations)—

(a) if an officer of the enforcer reasonably suspects a breach of the Electromagnetic Compatibility Regulations 2006 (SI 2006/3418), and

(b) for the purpose of ascertaining (by means of testing or otherwise) whether there has been such a breach.

(8) For the purposes of the enforcement of the Estate Agents Act 1979—

(a) the references in sub-paragraphs (2) and (3)(a) to ascertaining compliance with the enforcer's legislation include ascertaining whether a person has engaged in a practice mentioned in section 3(1)(d) of that Act (practice in relation to estate agency work declared undesirable by the Secretary of State), and

(b) the references in sub-paragraph (4) and paragraphs 23(6)(a) and 32(3)(a) to a breach of the enforcer's legislation include references to a person's engaging in such a practice.

Exercise of powers in this Part: EU enforcers

20 (1) Any power in this Part of this Schedule which is conferred on an EU enforcer may be exercised by such an enforcer only for the purposes and in the circumstances mentioned in this paragraph in relation to that power.

(2) If the condition in sub-paragraph (3) is met, an EU enforcer may exercise any power conferred on it by paragraphs 21 to 25 and 31 to 34 for any purpose relating to the functions that the enforcer has under Part 8 of the Enterprise Act 2002 in its capacity as a CPC enforcer under that Part.

(3) The condition is that an officer of the EU enforcer reasonably suspects—
(a) that there has been, or is likely to be, a Community infringement,
(b) a failure to comply with an enforcement order or an interim enforcement order made on the application of that enforcer,
(c) a failure to comply with an undertaking given under section 217(9) or 218(10) of the Enterprise Act 2002 following such an application, or
(d) a failure to comply with an undertaking given to that enforcer under section 219 of that Act.

(4) An EU enforcer may exercise the power in paragraph 27 (power to require the production of documents) for either of the following purposes—
(a) the purpose mentioned in sub-paragraph (2), if the condition in sub-paragraph (3) is met;
(b) to ascertain whether the documents may be required as evidence in proceedings under Part 8 of the Enterprise Act 2002.

(5) An EU enforcer may exercise the power in paragraph 28 (power to seize and detain goods) in relation to goods which an officer of the enforcer reasonably suspects—
(a) may disclose (by means of testing or otherwise) a Community infringement or a failure to comply with a measure specified in sub-paragraph (3)(b), (c) or (d), or
(b) may be required as evidence in proceedings under Part 8 of the Enterprise Act 2002.

(6) An EU enforcer may exercise the power in paragraph 29 (power to seize documents required as evidence) in relation to documents which an officer of the enforcer reasonably suspects may be required as evidence in proceedings under Part 8 of the Enterprise Act 2002.

Power to purchase products

21 (1) An officer of an enforcer may—
(a) make a purchase of a product, or
(b) enter into an agreement to secure the provision of a product.

(2) For the purposes of exercising the power in sub-paragraph (1), an officer may—
(a) at any reasonable time, enter premises to which the public has access (whether or not the public has access at that time), and
(b) inspect any product on the premises which the public may inspect.

(3) The power of entry in sub-paragraph (2) may be exercised without first giving notice or obtaining a warrant.

Power to observe carrying on of business etc

22 (1) An officer of an enforcer may enter premises to which the public has access in order to observe the carrying on of a business on those premises.

(2) The power in sub-paragraph (1) may be exercised at any reasonable time (whether or not the public has access at that time).

(3) The power of entry in sub-paragraph (1) may be exercised without first giving notice or obtaining a warrant.

Power to enter premises without warrant

23 (1) An officer of an enforcer may enter premises at any reasonable time.

(2) Sub-paragraph (1) does not authorise the entry into premises used wholly or mainly as a dwelling.

(3) In the case of a routine inspection, the power of entry in sub-paragraph (1) may only be exercised if a notice has been given to the occupier of the premises in accordance with the requirements in sub-paragraph (4), unless sub-paragraph (5) applies.

(4) Those requirements are that—

(a) the notice is in writing and is given by an officer of the enforcer,

(b) the notice sets out why the entry is necessary and indicates the nature of the offence under paragraph 36 (obstruction), and

(c) there are at least two working days between the date of receipt of the notice and the date of entry.

(5) A notice need not be given if the occupier has waived the requirement to give notice.

(6) In this paragraph "routine inspection" means an exercise of the power in sub-paragraph (1) other than where—

(a) the power is exercised by an officer of a domestic enforcer who reasonably suspects a breach of the enforcer's legislation,

(b) the officer reasonably considers that to give notice in accordance with sub-paragraph (3) would defeat the purpose of the entry,

(c) it is not reasonably practicable in all the circumstances to give notice in accordance with that sub-paragraph, in particular because the officer reasonably suspects that there is an imminent risk to public health or safety, or

(d) the enforcer is a market surveillance authority within the meaning of Article 2(18) of the Regulation on Accreditation and Market Surveillance and the entry is for the purpose of market surveillance within the meaning of Article 2(17) of that Regulation.

(7) If an officer of an enforcer enters premises under sub-paragraph (1) otherwise than in the course of a routine inspection, and finds one or more occupiers on the premises, the officer must provide to that occupier or (if there is more than one) to at least one of them a document that—

(a) sets out why the entry is necessary, and

(b) indicates the nature of the offence under paragraph 36 (obstruction).

(8) If an officer of an enforcer enters premises under sub-paragraph (1) and finds one or more occupiers on the premises, the officer must produce evidence of the officer's

identity and authority to that occupier or (if there is more than one) to at least one of them.

(9) An officer need not comply with sub-paragraph (7) or (8) if it is not reasonably practicable to do so.

(10) Proceedings resulting from the exercise of the power under sub-paragraph (1) are not invalid merely because of a failure to comply with sub-paragraph (7) or (8).

(11) An officer entering premises under sub-paragraph (1) may be accompanied by such persons, and may take onto the premises such equipment, as the officer thinks necessary.

(12) In this paragraph—

"give", in relation to the giving of a notice to the occupier of premises, includes delivering or leaving it at the premises or sending it there by post;

"working day" means a day other than—

(a) Saturday or Sunday,

(b) Christmas Day or Good Friday, or

(c) a day which is a bank holiday under the Banking and Financial Dealings Act 1971 in the part of the United Kingdom in which the premises are situated.

Application of paragraphs 25 to 31

24 Paragraphs 25 to 31 apply if an officer of an enforcer has entered any premises under the power in paragraph 23(1) or under a warrant under paragraph 32.

Power to inspect products etc

25 (1) The officer may inspect any product on the premises.

(2) The power in sub-paragraph (3) is also available to an officer of a domestic enforcer acting pursuant to the duty in section 27(1) of the Consumer Protection Act 1987 or regulation 10(1) of the General Product Safety Regulations 2005 (SI 2005/1803).

(3) The officer may examine any procedure (including any arrangements for carrying out a test) connected with the production of a product.

(4) The powers in sub-paragraph (5) are also available to an officer of a domestic enforcer acting pursuant to—

(a) the duty in regulation 10(1) of the Weights and Measures (Packaged Goods) Regulations 2006 (SI 2006/659) ("the ("2006 Regulations"), or

(b) the duty in regulation 10(1) of the Weights and Measures (Packaged Goods) Regulations (Northern Ireland) 2011 (SR 2011/331) ("the 2011 Regulations").

(5) The officer may inspect and take copies of, or of anything purporting to be—

(a) a record of a kind mentioned in regulation 5(2) or 9(1), or

(b) evidence of a kind mentioned in regulation 9(3).

(6) The references in sub-paragraph (5) to regulations are to regulations in the 2006 Regulations in the case of a domestic enforcer in Great Britain or the 2011 Regulations in the case of a domestic enforcer in Northern Ireland.

(7) The powers in sub-paragraph (8) are also available to an officer of a domestic enforcer acting pursuant to the duty in regulation 37(1)(a)(ii) or (b)(ii) of the Electromagnetic Compatibility Regulations 2006 (SI 2006/3418).

(8) The officer may—

(a) inspect any apparatus or fixed installation (as defined in those Regulations), or

(b) examine any procedure (including any arrangements for carrying out a test) connected with the production of apparatus.

Power to test equipment

26 (1) An officer of a domestic enforcer may test any weighing or measuring equipment—

(a) which is, or which the officer has reasonable cause to believe may be, used for trade or in the possession of any person or on any premises for such use, or

(b) which has been, or which the officer has reasonable cause to believe to have been, passed by an approved verifier, or by a person purporting to act as such a verifier, as fit for such use.

(2) Expressions used in sub-paragraph (1) have the same meaning—

(a) as in the Weights and Measures Act 1985, in the case of a domestic enforcer in Great Britain;

(b) as in the Weights and Measures (Northern Ireland) Order 1981 (SI 1981/231 (NI 10)), in the case of a domestic enforcer in Northern Ireland.

(3) The powers in sub-paragraph (4) are available to an officer of a domestic enforcer acting pursuant to—

(a) the duty in regulation 10(1) of the Weights and Measures (Packaged Goods) Regulations 2006 (SI 2006/659) ("the 2006 Regulations"), or

(b) the duty in regulation 10(1) of the Weights and Measures (Packaged Goods) Regulations (Northern Ireland) 2011 (SR 2011/331) ("the 2011 Regulations").

(4) The officer may test any equipment which the officer has reasonable cause to believe is used in—

(a) making up packages (as defined in regulation 2) in the United Kingdom, or

(b) carrying out a check mentioned in paragraphs (1) and (3) of regulation 9.

(5) The references in sub-paragraph (4) to regulations are to regulations in the 2006 Regulations in the case of a domestic enforcer in Great Britain or the 2011 Regulations in the case of a domestic enforcer in Northern Ireland.

Power to require the production of documents

27 (1) The officer may, at any reasonable time—

(a) require a trader occupying the premises, or a person on the premises acting on behalf of such a trader, to produce any documents relating to the trader's business to which the trader has access, and

(b) take copies of, or of any entry in, any such document.

(2) The power in sub-paragraph (1) is available regardless of whether—

(a) the purpose for which the documents are required relates to the trader or some other person, or

(b) the proceedings referred to in paragraph 19(3)(b) or 20(4)(b) could be taken against the trader or some other person.

(3) That power includes power to require the person to give an explanation of the documents.

(4) Where a document required to be produced under sub-paragraph (1) contains information recorded electronically, the power in that sub-paragraph includes power to require the production of a copy of the document in a form in which it can easily be taken away and in which it is visible and legible.

(5) This paragraph does not permit an officer to require a person to create a document other than as described in sub-paragraph (4).

(6) This paragraph does not permit an officer to require a person to produce any document which the person would be entitled to refuse to produce—

(a) in proceedings in the High Court on the grounds of legal professional privilege, or

(b) in proceedings in the Court of Session on the grounds of confidentiality of communications.

(7) In sub-paragraph (6) "communications" means—

(a) communications between a professional legal adviser and the adviser's client, or

(b) communications made in connection with or in contemplation of legal proceedings or for the purposes of those proceedings.

(8) In this paragraph "trader" has the same meaning as in Part 1 of this Act.

Power to seize and detain goods

28 (1) The officer may seize and detain goods other than documents (for which see paragraph 29).

(2) An officer seizing goods under this paragraph from premises which are occupied must produce evidence of the officer's identity and authority to an occupier of the premises before seizing them.

(3) The officer need not comply with sub-paragraph (2) if it is not reasonably practicable to do so.

(4) An officer seizing goods under this paragraph must take reasonable steps to—

(a) inform the person from whom they are seized that they have been seized, and

(b) provide that person with a written record of what has been seized.

(5) If, under this paragraph, an officer seizes any goods from a vending machine, the duty in sub-paragraph (4) also applies in relation to—

(a) the person whose name and address are on the vending machine as the owner of the machine, or

(b) if there is no such name and address on the machine, the occupier of the premises on which the machine stands or to which it is fixed.

(6) In determining the steps to be taken under sub-paragraph (4), an officer exercising a power under this paragraph in England and Wales or Northern Ireland must have regard to any relevant provision about the seizure of property made by—

(a) a code of practice under section 66 of the Police and Criminal Evidence Act 1984, or

(b) a code of practice under Article 65 of the Police and Criminal Evidence (Northern Ireland) Order 1989 (SI 1989/1341 (NI 12)),

(as the case may be).

(7) Goods seized under this paragraph (except goods seized for a purpose mentioned in paragraph 19(5)(b)) may not be detained—

(a) for a period of more than 3 months beginning with the day on which they were seized, or

(b) where the goods are reasonably required to be detained for a longer period by the enforcer for a purpose for which they were seized, for longer than they are required for that purpose.

Power to seize documents required as evidence

29 (1) The officer may seize and detain documents.

(2) An officer seizing documents under this paragraph from premises which are occupied must produce evidence of the officer's identity and authority to an occupier of the premises before seizing them.

(3) The officer need not comply with sub-paragraph (2) if it is not reasonably practicable to do so.

(4) An officer seizing documents under this paragraph must take reasonable steps to—

(a) inform the person from whom they are seized that they have been seized, and

(b) provide that person with a written record of what has been seized.

(5) In determining the steps to be taken under sub-paragraph (4), an officer exercising a power under this paragraph in England and Wales or Northern Ireland must have regard to any relevant provision about the seizure of property made by—

(a) a code of practice under section 66 of the Police and Criminal Evidence Act 1984, or

(b) a code of practice under Article 65 of the Police and Criminal Evidence (Northern Ireland) Order 1989 (SI 1989/1341 (NI 12)),

(as the case may be).

(6) This paragraph does not confer any power on an officer to seize from a person any document which the person would be entitled to refuse to produce—

(a) in proceedings in the High Court on the grounds of legal professional privilege, or

(b) in proceedings in the Court of Session on the grounds of confidentiality of communications.

(7) In sub-paragraph (6) "communications" means—

(a) communications between a professional legal adviser and the adviser's client, or

(b) communications made in connection with or in contemplation of legal proceedings or for the purposes of those proceedings.

(8) Documents seized under this paragraph may not be detained—

(a) for a period of more than 3 months beginning with the day on which they were seized, or

(b) where the documents are reasonably required to be detained for a longer period by the enforcer for the purposes of the proceedings for which they were seized, for longer than they are required for those purposes.

Power to decommission or switch off fixed installations

30 (1) The power in sub-paragraph (2) is available to an officer of a domestic enforcer acting pursuant to the duty in regulation 37(1)(a)(ii) or (b)(ii) of the Electromagnetic Compatibility Regulations 2006 (SI 2006/3418).

(2) The officer may decommission or switch off any fixed installation (as defined in those Regulations) or part of such an installation.

Power to break open container etc

31 (1) The officer may, for the purpose of exercising any of the powers in paragraphs 28 to 30, require a person with authority to do so to—

(a) break open any container,

(b) open any vending machine, or

(c) access any electronic device in which information may be stored or from which it may be accessed.

(2) Where a requirement under sub-paragraph (1) has not been complied with, the officer may, for the purpose of exercising any of the powers in paragraphs 28 to 30—

(a) break open the container,

(b) open the vending machine, or

(c) access the electronic device.

(3) Sub-paragraph (1) or (2) applies if and to the extent that the exercise of the power in that sub-paragraph is reasonably necessary for the purposes for which that power may be exercised.

(4) In this paragraph "container" means anything in which goods may be stored.

Power to enter premises with warrant

32 (1) A justice of the peace may issue a warrant authorising an officer of an enforcer to enter premises if satisfied, on written information on oath given by such an officer, that there are reasonable grounds for believing that—

(a) condition A or B is met, and

(b) condition C, D or E is met.

(2) Condition A is that on the premises there are—

(a) products which an officer of the enforcer has power to inspect under paragraph 25, or

(b) documents which an officer of the enforcer could require a person to produce under paragraph 27.

(3) Condition B is that, on the premises—

(a) in the case of a domestic enforcer, there has been or is about to be a breach of the enforcer's legislation,

(b) in the case of an EU enforcer, there has been or is about to be a Community infringement as defined in section 212 of the Enterprise Act 2002, or

(c) in the case of an EU enforcer, there has been a failure to comply with a measure specified in paragraph 20(3)(b), (c) or (d).

(4) Condition C is that—

(a) access to the premises has been or is likely to be refused, and

(b) notice of the enforcer's intention to apply for a warrant under this paragraph has been given to the occupier of the premises.

(5) Condition D is that it is likely that products or documents on the premises would be concealed or interfered with if notice of entry on the premises were given to the occupier of the premises.

(6) Condition E is that—

(a) the premises are unoccupied, or

(b) the occupier of the premises is absent, and it might defeat the purpose of the entry to wait for the occupier's return.

(7) In the application of this paragraph to Scotland—

(a) the reference in sub-paragraph (1) to a justice of the peace is to be read as a reference to a sheriff, and

(b) the reference in that sub-paragraph to information on oath is to be read as a reference to evidence on oath.

(8) In the application of this paragraph to Northern Ireland—

(a) the reference in sub-paragraph (1) to a justice of the peace is to be read as a reference to a lay magistrate, and

(b) the reference in that sub-paragraph to written information is to be read as a reference to a written complaint.

Entry to premises under warrant

33 (1) A warrant under paragraph 32 authorises an officer of the enforcer to enter the premises at any reasonable time, using reasonable force if necessary.

(2) A warrant under that paragraph ceases to have effect at the end of the period of one month beginning with the day it is issued.

(3) An officer entering premises under a warrant under paragraph 32 may be accompanied by such persons, and may take onto the premises such equipment, as the officer thinks necessary.

(4) If the premises are occupied when the officer enters them, the officer must produce the warrant for inspection to an occupier of the premises.

(5) Sub-paragraph (6) applies if the premises are unoccupied or the occupier is temporarily absent.

(6) On leaving the premises the officer must—

(a) leave a notice on the premises stating that the premises have been entered under a warrant under paragraph 32, and

(b) leave the premises as effectively secured against trespassers as the officer found them.

Power to require assistance from person on premises

34 (1) If an officer of an enforcer has entered premises under the power in paragraph 23(1) or under a warrant under paragraph 32, the officer may require any person on the premises to provide such assistance or information as the officer reasonably considers necessary.

(2) Sub-paragraph (3) applies if an officer of a domestic enforcer has entered premises under the power in paragraph 23(1) or under a warrant under paragraph 32 for the purposes of the enforcement of—

(a) the Weights and Measures (Packaged Goods) Regulations 2006 (SI 2006/659), or

(b) the Weights and Measures (Packaged Goods) Regulations (Northern Ireland) 2011 (SR 2011/331).

(3) The officer may, in particular, require any person on the premises to provide such information as the person possesses about the name and address of the packer and of any importer of a package which the officer finds on the premises.

(4) In sub-paragraph (3) "importer", "package" and "packer" have the same meaning as in—

(a) the Weights and Measures (Packaged Goods) Regulations 2006 (see regulation 2), in the case of a domestic enforcer in Great Britain, or

(b) the Weights and Measures (Packaged Goods) Regulations (Northern Ireland) 2011 (see regulation 2), in the case of a domestic enforcer in Northern Ireland.

Definitions for purposes of this Part

35 In this Part of this Schedule—

"goods" has the meaning given by section 2(8);

"occupier", in relation to premises, means any person an officer of an enforcer reasonably suspects to be the occupier of the premises;

"premises" includes any stall, vehicle, vessel or aircraft;

"product" means—

(a) goods,

(b) a service,

(c) digital content, as defined in section 2(9),

(d) immovable property, or

(e) rights or obligations.

PART 5

PROVISIONS SUPPLEMENTARY TO PARTS 3 AND 4

Offence of obstruction

36 (1) A person commits an offence if the person—

(a) intentionally obstructs an enforcer or an officer of an enforcer who is exercising or seeking to exercise a power under Part 4 of this Schedule in accordance with that Part,

(b) intentionally fails to comply with a requirement properly imposed by an enforcer or an officer of an enforcer under Part 4 of this Schedule, or

(c) without reasonable cause fails to give an enforcer or an officer of an enforcer any other assistance or information which the enforcer or officer reasonably requires of the person for a purpose for which the enforcer or officer may exercise a power under Part 4 of this Schedule.

(2) A person commits an offence if, in giving information of a kind referred to in sub-paragraph (1)(c), the person—

(a) makes a statement which the person knows is false or misleading in a material respect, or

(b) recklessly makes a statement which is false or misleading in a material respect.

(3) A person who is guilty of an offence under sub-paragraph (1) or (2) is liable on summary conviction to a fine not exceeding level 3 on the standard scale.

(4) Nothing in this paragraph requires a person to answer any question or give any information if to do so might incriminate that person.

Offence of purporting to act as officer

37 (1) A person who is not an officer of an enforcer commits an offence if the person purports to act as such under Part 3 or 4 of this Schedule.

(2) A person who is guilty of an offence under sub-paragraph (1) is liable on summary conviction to a fine not exceeding level 5 on the standard scale.

(3) If section 85(1) of the Legal Aid, Sentencing and Punishment of Offenders Act 2012 comes into force on or before the day on which this Act is passed—

(a) section 85 of that Act (removal of limit on certain fines on conviction by magistrates' court) applies in relation to the offence in this paragraph as if it were a relevant offence (as defined in section 85(3) of that Act), and

(b) regulations described in section 85(11) of that Act may amend or otherwise modify sub-paragraph (2).

Access to seized goods and documents

38 (1) This paragraph applies where anything seized by an officer of an enforcer under Part 4 of this Schedule is detained by the enforcer.

(2) If a request for permission to be granted access to that thing is made to the enforcer by a person who had custody or control of it immediately before it was seized, the

enforcer must allow that person access to it under the supervision of an officer of the enforcer.

(3) If a request for a photograph or copy of that thing is made to the enforcer by a person who had custody or control of it immediately before it was seized, the enforcer must—

(a) allow that person access to it under the supervision of an officer of the enforcer for the purpose of photographing or copying it, or

(b) photograph or copy it, or cause it to be photographed or copied.

(4) Where anything is photographed or copied under sub-paragraph (3), the photograph or copy must be supplied to the person who made the request within a reasonable time from the making of the request.

(5) This paragraph does not require access to be granted to, or a photograph or copy to be supplied of, anything if the enforcer has reasonable grounds for believing that to do so would prejudice the investigation for the purposes of which it was seized.

(6) An enforcer may recover the reasonable costs of complying with a request under this paragraph from the person by whom or on whose behalf it was made.

(7) References in this paragraph to a person who had custody or control of a thing immediately before it was seized include a representative of such a person.

Notice of testing of goods

39 (1) Sub-paragraphs (3) and (4) apply where goods purchased by an officer of a domestic enforcer under paragraph 21 are submitted to a test and as a result—

(a) proceedings are brought for a breach of, or under, the enforcer's legislation or for the forfeiture of the goods by the enforcer, or

(b) a notice is served by the enforcer preventing a person from doing any thing.

(2) Sub-paragraphs (3) and (4) also apply where goods seized by an officer of a domestic enforcer under paragraph 28 are submitted to a test.

(3) The enforcer must inform the relevant person of the results of the test.

(4) The enforcer must allow a relevant person to have the goods tested if it is reasonably practicable to do so.

(5) In sub-paragraph (3) "relevant person" means the person from whom the goods were purchased or seized or, where the goods were purchased or seized from a vending machine—

(a) the person whose name and address are on the vending machine as the owner of the machine, or

(b) if there is no such name and address on the machine, the occupier of the premises on which the machine stands or to which it is fixed.

(6) In sub-paragraph (4) "relevant person" means—

(a) a person within sub-paragraph (5),

(b) in a case within sub-paragraph (1)(a), a person who is a party to the proceedings, and

(c) in a case within sub-paragraph (1)(b), a person with an interest in the goods.

Appeals against detention of goods and documents

40 (1) This paragraph applies where goods or documents are being detained as the result of the exercise of a power in Part 4 of this Schedule.

(2) A person with an interest in the goods or documents may apply for an order requiring them to be released to that or another person.

(3) An application under this paragraph may be made in England and Wales or Northern Ireland—

(a) to any magistrates' court in which proceedings have been brought for an offence as the result of the investigation in the course of which the goods or documents were seized,

(b) to any magistrates' court in which proceedings have been brought for the forfeiture of the goods or documents or (in the case of seized documents) any goods to which the documents relate, or

(c) if no proceedings within paragraph (a) or (b) have been brought, by way of complaint to a magistrates' court.

(4) An application under this paragraph may be made in Scotland by summary application to the sheriff.

(5) On an application under this paragraph, the court or sheriff may make an order requiring goods to be released only if satisfied that condition A or B is met.

(6) Condition A is that—

(a) no proceedings have been brought—

(i) for an offence as the result of the investigation in the course of which the goods or documents were seized, or

(ii) for the forfeiture of the goods or documents or (in the case of seized documents) any goods to which the documents relate, and

(b) the period of 6 months beginning with the date the goods or documents were seized has expired.

(7) Condition B is that—

(a) proceedings of a kind mentioned in sub-paragraph (6)(a) have been brought, and

(b) those proceedings have been concluded without the goods or documents being forfeited.

(8) A person aggrieved by an order made under this paragraph by a magistrates' court, or by the decision of a magistrates' court not to make such an order, may appeal against the order or decision—

(a) in England and Wales, to the Crown Court;

(b) in Northern Ireland, to a county court.

(9) An order made under this paragraph by a magistrates' court may contain such provision as the court thinks appropriate for delaying its coming into force pending the making and determination of any appeal.

(10) In sub-paragraph (9) "appeal" includes an application under section 111 of the Magistrates' Courts Act 1980 or Article 146 of the Magistrates' Courts (Northern Ireland) Order 1981 (SI 1981/1675 (NI 26)) (statements of case).

Compensation

41 (1) This paragraph applies where an officer of an enforcer has seized and detained goods under Part 4 of this Schedule for a purpose within paragraph 19(5)(a) or 20(5)(a).

(2) The enforcer must pay compensation to any person with an interest in the goods in respect of any loss or damage caused by the seizure and detention, if the condition in sub-paragraph (3) or (4) that is relevant to the enforcer is met.

(3) The condition that is relevant to a domestic enforcer is that—

(a) the goods have not disclosed a breach of the enforcer's legislation, and

(b) the power to seize and detain the goods was not exercised as a result of any neglect or default of the person seeking the compensation.

(4) The condition that is relevant to an EU enforcer is that—

(a) the goods have not disclosed a Community infringement or a failure to comply with a measure specified in paragraph 20(3)(b), (c) or (d), and

(b) the power to seize and detain the goods was not exercised as a result of any neglect or default of the person seeking the compensation.

(5) Any dispute about the right to or amount of any compensation payable under this paragraph is to be determined—

(a) in England and Wales or Northern Ireland, by arbitration, or

(b) in Scotland, by a single arbitrator appointed by the parties or, if there is no agreement between the parties as to that appointment, by the sheriff.

Meaning of "goods" in this Part

42 In this Part of this Schedule "goods" does not include a document.

PART 6

EXERCISE OF ENFORCEMENT FUNCTIONS BY AREA ENFORCERS

Interpretation of this Part

43 In this Part, "area enforcer" means—

(a) a local weights and measures authority in Great Britain,

(b) a district council in England, or

(c) a district council in Northern Ireland.

Investigatory powers

44 (1) Sub-paragraphs (3) to (6) apply in relation to an area enforcer's exercise, in accordance with this Schedule, of a power in Part 3 or 4 of this Schedule.

(2) Sub-paragraphs (3) to (6) also apply in relation to an area enforcer's exercise of an investigatory power—

(a) conferred by legislation which, by virtue of a provision listed in paragraph 10 of this Schedule, the area enforcer has a duty or power to enforce, or conferred by legislation under which such legislation is made, or

(b) conferred by legislation listed in the second column of the table in paragraph 11 of this Schedule,

for the purpose of ascertaining whether there has been a breach of that legislation or of any notice issued by the area enforcer under that legislation.

(3) A local weights and measures authority in England or Wales may exercise the power in a part of England or Wales which is outside that authority's area.

(4) A local weights and measures authority in Scotland may exercise the power in a part of Scotland which is outside that authority's area.

(5) A district council in England may exercise the power in a part of England which is outside that council's district.

(6) A district council in Northern Ireland may exercise the power in a part of Northern Ireland which is outside that council's district.

Civil proceedings

45 (1) Sub-paragraphs (4) to (7) apply in relation to civil proceedings which may be brought by an area enforcer under—

(a) Part 8 of the Enterprise Act 2002,

(b) Schedule 3 to this Act,

(c) legislation which, by virtue of a provision listed in paragraph 10 of this Schedule, the area enforcer has a duty or power to enforce,

(d) legislation under which legislation mentioned in paragraph (c) is made, or

(e) legislation listed in the second column of the table in paragraph 11 of this Schedule.

(2) Sub-paragraphs (4) to (7) also apply in relation to an application for forfeiture which may be made by an area enforcer, in circumstances where there are no related criminal proceedings,—

(a) under section 35ZC of the Registered Designs Act 1949,

(b) under section 16 of the Consumer Protection Act 1987,

(c) under section 97 of the Trade Marks Act 1994 (including as applied by section 11 of the Olympic Symbol etc (Protection) Act 1995), or

(d) under legislation which, by virtue of a provision listed in paragraph 10 of this Schedule, the area enforcer has a duty or power to enforce.

(3) In sub-paragraphs (4), (5), (6) and (7), the reference to civil proceedings includes a reference to an application mentioned in sub-paragraph (2).

(4) A local weights and measures authority in England or Wales may bring civil proceedings in respect of conduct in a part of England or Wales which is outside that authority's area.

(5) A local weights and measures authority in Scotland may bring civil proceedings in respect of conduct in a part of Scotland which is outside that authority's area.

(6) A district council in England may bring civil proceedings in respect of conduct in a part of England which is outside that council's district.

(7) A district council in Northern Ireland may bring civil proceedings in respect of conduct in a part of Northern Ireland which is outside that council's district.

Criminal proceedings

46 (1) A local weights and measures authority in England or Wales may bring proceedings for a consumer offence allegedly committed in a part of England or Wales which is outside that authority's area.

(2) In sub-paragraph (1) "a consumer offence" means—

(a) an offence under legislation which, by virtue of a provision listed in paragraph 10 of this Schedule, a local weights and measures authority in England or Wales has a duty or power to enforce,

(b) an offence under legislation under which legislation within paragraph (a) is made,

(c) an offence under legislation listed in the second column of the table in paragraph 11 of this Schedule in relation to which a local weights and measures authority is listed in the corresponding entry in the first column of the table as an enforcer,

(d) an offence originating from an investigation into a breach of legislation mentioned in paragraph (a), (b) or (c), or

(e) an offence described in paragraph 36 or 37 of this Schedule.

(3) A district council in England may bring proceedings for a consumer offence allegedly committed in a part of England which is outside that council's district.

(4) In sub-paragraph (3) "a consumer offence" means—

(a) an offence under legislation which, by virtue of a provision listed in paragraph 10 of this Schedule, a district council in England has a duty or power to enforce,

(b) an offence under legislation under which legislation within paragraph (a) is made,

(c) an offence originating from an investigation into a breach of legislation mentioned in paragraph (a) or (b), or

(d) an offence described in paragraph 36 or 37 of this Schedule.

(5) A district council in Northern Ireland may bring proceedings for a consumer offence allegedly committed in a part of Northern Ireland which is outside that council's district.

(6) In sub-paragraph (5) "a consumer offence" means—

(a) an offence under legislation which, by virtue of a provision listed in paragraph 10 of this Schedule, a district council in Northern Ireland has a duty or power to enforce,

(b) an offence under legislation under which legislation within paragraph (a) is made,

(c) an offence originating from an investigation into a breach of legislation mentioned in paragraph (a) or (b), or

(d) an offence described in paragraph 36 or 37 of this Schedule.

SCHEDULE 6

Section 77

INVESTIGATORY POWERS: CONSEQUENTIAL AMENDMENTS

Registered Designs Act 1949 (c. 88)

1 (1) Section 35ZB of the Registered Designs Act 1949 (enforcement) is amended as follows.

(2) Omit subsection (1).

(3) Before subsection (2) insert—

"(1A) For the investigatory powers available to a local weights and measures authority or the Department of Enterprise, Trade and Investment in Northern Ireland for the purposes of the enforcement of section 35ZA, see Schedule 5 to the Consumer Rights Act 2015."

Trade Descriptions Act 1968 (c. 29)

2 The Trade Descriptions Act 1968 is amended as follows.

3 In section 26 (enforcing authorities) after subsection (1) insert—

"(1A) For the investigatory powers available to a local weights and measures authority for the purposes of the duty in subsection (1), see Schedule 5 to the Consumer Rights Act 2015."

4 Omit section 27 (power to make test purchases).

5 Omit section 28 (power to enter premises and inspect and seize goods and documents).

6 Omit section 29 (obstruction of authorised officers).

7 Omit section 30 (notice of test and intended prosecution).

8 Omit section 33 (compensation for loss, etc of goods seized under section 28).

9 (1) Section 40 (provisions as to Northern Ireland) is amended as follows.

(2) In subsection (1), omit paragraph (c).

(3) After subsection (1) insert—

"(1A) For the investigatory powers available to the Department of Enterprise, Trade and Investment in Northern Ireland for the purposes of the duty in subsection (1)(b), see Schedule 5 to the Consumer Rights Act 2015."

Hallmarking Act 1973 (c. 43)

10 (1) Section 9 of the Hallmarking Act 1973 (enforcement of Act) is amended as follows.

(2) After subsection (2) insert—

"(2A) For the investigatory powers available to a local weights and measures authority, the Council and an assay office for the purposes of the duty in subsection (1) and the power in subsection (2), see Schedule 5 to the Consumer Rights Act 2015."

(3) Omit subsections (3), (4) and (7).

Prices Act 1974 (c. 24)

11 (1) The Schedule to the Prices Act 1974 (enforcement) is amended as follows.

(2) Omit paragraphs 3, 7, 9 and 10.

(3) In paragraph 14(1) omit "and paragraph 10 above shall be omitted".

(4) After paragraph 14 insert—

"15 For the investigatory powers available to a local weights and measures authority or the Department of Enterprise, Trade and Investment in Northern Ireland for the purposes of the duty in paragraph 6, see Schedule 5 to the Consumer Rights Act 2015."

Consumer Credit Act 1974 (c. 39)

12 The Consumer Credit Act 1974 is amended as follows.

13 In section 161 (enforcement authorities), after subsection (1A) insert—

"(1B) For the investigatory powers available to a local weights and measures authority or the Department of Enterprise, Trade and Investment in Northern Ireland for the purposes of the duty in subsection (1), see Schedule 5 to the Consumer Rights Act 2015."

14 Omit section 162 (powers of entry and inspection).

15 Omit section 163 (compensation for loss).

16 Omit section 164 (power to make test purchases etc).

17 Omit section 165 (obstruction of authorised officers).

18 In Schedule 1 (prosecution and punishment of offences) omit the entries for sections 162(6), 165(1) and 165(2).

Estate Agents Act 1979 (c. 38)

19 The Estate Agents Act 1979 is amended as follows.

20 In section 3(1)(cb) (power to make orders prohibiting unfit persons from doing estate agency work: failure to comply with section 9(1) or 11(1A)(b)) for "section 9(1) or 11(1A)(b) below" substitute "paragraph 14 or 27 of Schedule 5 to the Consumer Rights Act 2015".

21 In section 9 (information for the lead enforcement authority) omit subsections (1) to (4).

22 Omit section 11 (powers of entry and inspection).

23 Omit section 11A (failure to produce information).

24 In section 26 (enforcement authorities), after subsection (1) insert—

"(1A) For the investigatory powers available to an authority for the purposes of the duty in subsection (1), see Schedule 5 to the Consumer Rights Act 2015."

25 Omit section 27 (obstruction and personation of authorised officers).

26 (1) Paragraph 14 of Schedule 2 (applications under sections 6(1) and 8(3)) is amended as follows.

(2) For "section 9 of this Act" substitute "paragraph 14 of Schedule 5 to the Consumer Rights Act 2015".

(3) Omit "or the production of documents".

Video Recordings Act 1984 (c. 39)

27 (1) Section 16A of the Video Recordings Act 1984 (enforcement) is amended as follows.

(2) Omit subsections (1A), (1B) and (2).

(3) In subsection (4)—

(a) for "Subsections (1) and (1A)" substitute "Subsection (1)", and

(b) omit the words from "For that purpose" to the end of the subsection.

(4) After that subsection insert—

"(4ZA) For the investigatory powers available to a local weights and measures authority or the Department of Enterprise, Trade and Investment in Northern Ireland for the purposes of the functions in this section, see Schedule 5 to the Consumer Rights Act 2015."

(5) Omit subsection (4A).

Weights and Measures Act 1985 (c. 72)

28 The Weights and Measures Act 1985 is amended as follows.

29 In section 38(2) (special powers of inspectors with respect to certain goods) for "section 79 below" substitute "Schedule 5 to the Consumer Rights Act 2015".

30 Omit section 42 (power to make test purchases).

31 Omit section 79 (general powers of inspection and entry).

32 Before section 80 insert—

"79A Investigatory powers

"79A Investigatory powers

For the investigatory powers available to a local weights and measures authority for the purposes of the enforcement of this Act, see Schedule 5 to the Consumer Rights Act 2015."

33 In section 80 omit "or the packaged goods regulations".

34 In section 81(1)(b) (failure to provide assistance or information) omit "or under this Part of this Act".

35 (1) Section 84 (penalties) is amended as follows.

(2) In subsection (2), after the entry for section 20(8) insert—

"section 80;

section 81(1);
section 81(2);".

(3) Omit subsection (5).

36 In paragraph 21(2)(b) of Schedule 11 (application of provisions applying to inspectors to persons authorised under the Weights and Measures Act 1963) omit "and except in section 79(3)".

Consumer Protection Act 1987 (c. 43)

37 The Consumer Protection Act 1987 is amended as follows.

38 In section 27 (enforcement) after subsection (3) insert—

"(3A) For the investigatory powers available to a person for the purposes of the duty imposed by subsection (1), see Schedule 5 to the Consumer Rights Act 2015 (as well as section 29)."

39 Omit section 28 (test purchases).

40 (1) Section 29 (powers of search etc) is amended as follows.

(2) In subsection (1) for "any of the powers conferred by the following provisions of this section" substitute "the power conferred by subsection (4)".

(3) Omit subsections (2), (3), (5) and (6).

(4) In subsection (7) omit—

(a) ", (5) or (6)", and
(b) "or records".

41 (1) Section 30 (provisions supplemental to section 29) is amended as follows.

(2) In subsection (1)—

(a) for "29" substitute "29(4)", and
(b) omit "or records" in both places.

(3) In subsection (2)(a)(i)—

(a) omit "goods or", and
(b) for "29" substitute "29(4)".

(4) In subsection (3) omit "section 29 above or".

(5) In each of subsections (5), (6) and (7) for "29" substitute "29(4)".

42 In section 31(1) (power of customs officer to detain goods) for "or under this Part" substitute "section 29(4) of this Act or Schedule 5 to the Consumer Rights Act 2015".

43 In section 32(1) (obstruction of authorised officer)—

(a) in paragraph (a)—
  (i) for "any provision of this Part" substitute "section 29(4)", and
  (ii) for "so acting" substitute "acting in pursuance of section 31",
(b) in paragraph (b) for "any provision of this Part" substitute "section 29(4)", and
(c) in paragraph (c) for "any provision of this Part" substitute "section 29(4)".

44 In section 33(1) (appeals against detention of goods) for "any provision of this Part" substitute "section 29(4)".

45 In section 34(1) (compensation for seizure and detention) for "29" substitute "29(4)".

46 In section 44(4) (service of documents)—

(a) omit "28(2) or", and

(b) omit "purchased or" in each place.

Education Reform Act 1988 (c. 40)

47 (1) Section 215 of the Education Reform Act 1988 (unrecognised degrees: enforcement) is amended as follows.

(2) After that section insert—

"(1A) For the investigatory powers available to a local weights and measures authority for the purposes of the duty to enforce imposed by subsection (1), see Schedule 5 to the Consumer Rights Act 2015."

(3) Omit subsections (2) to (8).

Copyright, Designs and Patents Act 1988 (c. 48)

48 The Copyright, Designs and Patents Act 1988 is amended as follows.

49 (1) Section 107A (enforcement of section 107 by local weights and measures authority) is amended as follows.

(2) Omit subsection (2).

(3) In subsection (3) omit the words from "For that purpose" to the end of the subsection.

(4) After that subsection insert—

"(3A) For the investigatory powers available to a local weights and measures authority or the Department of Enterprise, Trade and Investment in Northern Ireland for the purposes of the duties in this section, see Schedule 5 to the Consumer Rights Act 2015."

50 (1) Section 198A (enforcement of section 198 by local weights and measures authority) is amended as follows.

(2) Omit subsection (2).

(3) In subsection (3) omit the words from "For that purpose" to the end of the subsection.

(4) After that subsection insert—

"(3A) For the investigatory powers available to a local weights and measures authority or the Department of Enterprise, Trade and Investment in Northern Ireland for the purposes of the duties in this section, see Schedule 5 to the Consumer Rights Act 2015."

Clean Air Act 1993 (c. 11)

51 The Clean Air Act 1993 is amended as follows.

52 (1) Section 30 (regulations about motor fuel) is amended as follows.

(2) Omit subsection (5).

(3) Before subsection (6) insert—

"(5A) For the investigatory powers available to a local weights and measures authority for the purposes of the duty in subsection (4), see Schedule 5 to the Consumer Rights Act 2015."

(4) Omit subsection (8).

(5) Before subsection (9) insert—

"(8A) For the investigatory powers available to the Department of Enterprise, Trade and Investment in Northern Ireland for the purposes of the duty in subsection (7), see Schedule 5 to the Consumer Rights Act 2015."

53 In section 31 (regulations about sulphur content of oil fuel for furnaces or engines) after subsection (4) insert—

"(4A) For the investigatory powers available to a local authority for the purposes of the duty in subsection (4)(a), see Schedule 5 to the Consumer Rights Act 2015."

54 In section 32(4) (powers of entry not to apply in relation to persons in the public service of the Crown) for "sections 56 to 58 (rights of entry and inspection and other local authority powers)" substitute "Schedule 5 to the Consumer Rights Act 2015 (investigatory powers)".

55 In section 49(1) (unjustified disclosures of information) after "this Act" insert "or in the exercise of a power in Schedule 5 to the Consumer Rights Act 2015 for the purposes of the duty in section 30(4) or (7) or 31(4)(a) of this Act".

56 In section 56 (rights of entry and inspection etc) after subsection (6) insert—

"(7) This section does not apply in relation to—
(a) a function conferred on a local authority by Part 4, or
(b) a provision of an instrument made under that Part."

57 In section 58(1) (power of local authorities to obtain information)—
(a) omit "IV or", and
(b) for "those Parts" substitute "that Part".

Sunday Trading Act 1994 (c. 20)

58 (1) Part 1 of Schedule 2 to the Sunday Trading Act 1994 (general enforcement provisions) is amended as follows.

(2) Omit paragraphs 3 and 4.

(3) Before paragraph 5 insert—

"4A Investigatory powers

4A For the investigatory powers available to a local authority and the inspectors appointed by it under paragraph 2 for the purposes of the duty in paragraph 1, see Schedule 5 to the Consumer Rights Act 2015."

Trade Marks Act 1994 (c. 26)

59 (1) Section 93 of the Trade Marks Act 1994 (enforcement function of local weights and measures authority) is amended as follows.

(2) Omit subsection (2).

(3) In subsection (3) omit the words from "For that purpose" to the end of the subsection.

(4) After that subsection insert—

"(3A) For the investigatory powers available to a local weights and measures authority or the Department of Enterprise, Trade and Investment in Northern Ireland for the purposes of the duties in this section, see Schedule 5 to the Consumer Rights Act 2015."

Olympic Symbol etc (Protection) Act 1995 (c. 32)

60 (1) Section 8A of the Olympic Symbol etc (Protection) Act 1995 is amended as follows.

(2) Omit subsection (2).

(3) In subsection (3) omit paragraph (b) and the "and" immediately preceding that paragraph.

(4) After that subsection insert—

"(3A) For the investigatory powers available to a local weights and measures authority or the Department of Enterprise, Trade and Investment in Northern Ireland for the purposes of the powers in this section, see Schedule 5 to the Consumer Rights Act 2015."

Criminal Justice and Police Act 2001 (c. 16)

61 The Criminal Justice and Police Act 2001 is amended as follows.

62 In section 57(1) (retention of seized items)—

(a) omit paragraphs (d), (g) and (pa), and

(b) after paragraph (r) insert—

"(s) paragraphs 28(7) and 29(8) of Schedule 5 to the Consumer Rights Act 2015".

63 (1) Section 65 (meaning of legal privilege) is amended as follows.

(2) Omit subsections (6) and (8A).

(3) Before subsection (9) insert—

"(8B) An item which is, or is comprised in, property which has been seized in exercise or purported exercise of the power of seizure conferred by paragraph 27(1)(b) or 29(1) of Schedule 5 to the Consumer Rights Act 2015 shall be taken for the purposes of this Part to be an item subject to legal privilege if, and only if, the seizure of that item was in contravention of paragraph 27(6) or (as the case may be) 29(6) of that Schedule (privileged documents)."

(4) In subsection (9)—

(a) omit paragraph (c),

(b) at the end of paragraph (d) insert "or", and
(c) omit paragraph (f) and the "or" immediately preceding that paragraph.

64 In section 66(4) (construction of references to a search)—
(a) omit paragraphs (a), (c), (d), (e), (f), (g), (ma), (q), (r) and (s),
(b) in paragraph (h) for "29" substitute "29(4)",
(c) in paragraph (o) for "22" substitute "22(4)", and
(d) after paragraph (p) insert—
"(t) Part 4 of Schedule 5 to the Consumer Rights Act 2015".

65 (1) Part 1 of Schedule 1 (powers to which section 50 applies) is amended as follows.

(2) Omit—
(a) paragraph 9,
(b) paragraph 16,
(c) paragraph 18,
(d) paragraph 19,
(e) paragraph 24,
(f) paragraph 36,
(g) paragraph 73BA,
(h) the first paragraph 73G,
(i) the second paragraph 73J,
(j) the second paragraph 73K,
(k) paragraph 73N, and
(l) paragraph 73O.

(3) In paragraph 45 for "29(4), (5) and (6)" substitute "29(4)".

(4) In the second paragraph 73G for "22(4) to (6)" substitute "22(4)".

(5) After paragraph 73M insert—

"73P Consumer Rights Act 2015

73P Each of the powers of seizure conferred by paragraphs 27(1)(b), 28(1) and 29(1) of Schedule 5 to the Consumer Rights Act 2015."

66 (1) Part 1 of Schedule 2 (application of enactments) is amended as follows.

(2) Omit paragraphs 1, 4B, 4C, 5, 7, 9B and 9C.

(3) In paragraph 3 for "29" in each place substitute "29(4)".

(4) In paragraph 4A—
(a) for "23" substitute "22(4)", and
(b) for "22" substitute "22(4)".

(5) After paragraph 4A insert—

"4D Paragraph 39 of Schedule 5 to the Consumer Rights Act 2015 (notice of testing of goods) shall apply in relation to items seized under section 50 of this Act in reliance on the power of seizure conferred by paragraph 28(1) of that Schedule as it applies in relation to goods seized under that paragraph.

4E Access to seized items

4E Subject to section 61 of this Act, paragraph 38 of Schedule 5 to the Consumer Rights Act 2015 (access to seized goods and documents) shall apply in relation to items seized under section 50 of this Act in reliance on the power of seizure conferred by paragraph 28(1) or 29(1) of that Schedule as it applies in relation to things seized under Part 4 of that Schedule."

(6) In paragraph 8 for "29" in each place substitute "29(4)".

(7) In paragraph 9A—

(a) for the first "22" substitute "22(4)", and

(b) for "products under regulations 22 of those Regulations." substitute "those items, as it applies to the seizure and detention of products under regulation 22(4) of those Regulations."

(8) After paragraph 9A insert—

"9D Paragraph 41 of Schedule 5 to the Consumer Rights Act 2015 (compensation for seizure and detention) shall apply in relation to the seizure of items under section 50 of this Act in reliance on the power of seizure conferred by paragraph 28(1) or 29(1) of that Schedule, and the retention of those items, as it applies in relation to the seizure and detention of goods under Part 4 of that Schedule."

Enterprise Act 2002 (c. 40)

67 The Enterprise Act 2002 is amended as follows.

68 Omit section 224 (power of CMA to require the provision of information).

69 Omit section 225 (power of other enforcer to require the provision of information).

70 Omit section 226 (procedure for notices requiring information).

71 Omit section 227 (enforcement of notices).

72 Omit section 227A (power to enter premises without warrant).

73 Omit section 227B (powers exercisable on the premises).

74 Omit section 227C (power to enter premises with warrant).

75 Omit section 227D (ancillary provisions about powers of entry).

76 Omit section 227E (obstructing, or failing to co-operate with, powers of entry).

77 Omit section 227F (retention of documents and goods).

78 Before section 228 (but after the italic heading "Miscellaneous") insert—

"223A Investigatory powers

"223A Investigatory powers

For the investigatory powers available to enforcers for the purposes of enforcers' functions under this Part, see Schedule 5 to the Consumer Rights Act 2015."

79 In section 228 (evidence) omit subsection (4).

80 In section 236 (application of Part 8 to Crown) omit subsection (2).

81 In Schedule 14 (specified functions for the purposes of Part 9 restrictions on disclosure), at the end insert—

"Paragraph 13(2), (3) or (7) of Schedule 5 to the Consumer Rights Act 2015."

Fireworks Act 2003 (c. 22)

82 (1) Section 12 of the Fireworks Act 2003 (enforcement) is amended as follows.

(2) In subsection (2)—

(a) omit paragraph (a), and

(b) in paragraph (b), for "29(1) to (5), (6)(a) and (7)" substitute "29(4) and (7)".

(3) After subsection (2) insert—

"(2A) For the investigatory powers available to a person for the purposes of the duty to enforce imposed by virtue of subsection (1) (in addition to the powers in Part 4 of the Consumer Protection Act 1987), see Schedule 5 to the Consumer Rights Act 2015."

Christmas Day (Trading) Act 2004 (c. 26)

83 (1) Section 3 of the Christmas Day (Trading) Act 2004 (enforcement) is amended as follows.

(2) Omit subsection (3).

(3) Before subsection (4) insert—

"(3A) For the powers available to a local authority and the inspectors appointed by it under subsection (3) for the purposes of the duty in subsection (1), see Schedule 5 to the Consumer Rights Act 2015."

Financial Services Act 2012 (c. 21)

84 (1) Section 107 of the Financial Services Act 2012 (power to make further provision about regulation of consumer credit) is amended as follows.

(2) In subsection (2) omit paragraph (g).

(3) In subsection (4) for "(2)(g) to (i)" substitute "(2)(h) and (i)".

Consequential repeals and revocations

85 In consequence of the amendments made by this Schedule, the following are repealed or revoked—

(a) section 16(2)(b) of the Price Commission Act 1977;

(b) article 2(13) of the Deregulation (Weights and Measures) Order 1999 (SI 1999/503);

(c) paragraph 9(8)(b) and (9)(a) of Schedule 25 to the Enterprise Act 2002;

(d) paragraphs 50 and 62 of Schedule 27 to the Civil Partnerships Act 2004;

(e) paragraphs (10) and (24) to (27) of Schedule 1 to the Weights and Measures (Packaged Goods) Regulations 2006 (SI 2006/659);
(f) regulations 15 to 18 and 24 to 28 of the Enterprise Act 2002 (Amendment) Regulations 2006 (SI 2006/3363);
(g) section 51(2) of the Consumer Credit Act 2006;
(h) paragraph 41 of Schedule 21 to the Legal Services Act 2007;
(i) sections 57 and 58(1), (3) and (4) of the Consumers, Estate Agents and Redress Act 2007;
(j) paragraphs 63 to 65 of Schedule 2 to the Consumer Protection from Unfair Trading Regulations 2008 (SI 2008/1277);
(k) paragraph 2 of Schedule 6 to the Timeshare, Holiday Products, Resale and Exchange Contracts Regulations 2010 (SI 2010/2960);
(l) regulation 2 of the Timeshare (Amendment) Regulations 2011 (SI 2011/1065);
(m) paragraphs 17 to 20 of Schedule 1 to the Weights and Measures (Packaged Goods) Regulations (Northern Ireland) 2011 (SR 2011/331);
(n) paragraph 82(a) of Schedule 9 to the Crime and Courts Act 2013.

SCHEDULE 7

Section 79

ENTERPRISE ACT 2002: ENHANCED CONSUMER MEASURES AND OTHER ENFORCEMENT

1 Part 8 of the Enterprise Act 2002 (enforcement of certain consumer legislation) is amended as follows.

2 In section 210 (consumers), omit subsection (5).

3 (1) Section 211 (domestic infringements) is amended as follows.

(2) In subsection (1)(c), omit "in the United Kingdom".

(3) After subsection (1) insert—

"(1A) But an act or omission which satisfies the conditions in subsection (1) is a domestic infringement only if at least one of the following is satisfied—
(a) the person supplying (or seeking to supply) goods or services has a place of business in the United Kingdom, or
(b) the goods or services are supplied (or sought to be supplied) to or for a person in the United Kingdom (see section 232)."

4 In section 213(5A) (CPC enforcers), for paragraph (i) substitute—
"(i) an enforcement authority within the meaning of section 120(15) of the Communications Act 2003 (regulation of premium rate services);".

5 (1) Section 214 (consultation) is amended as follows.

(2) In subsection (4)(a), after "14 days" insert "or, where subsection (4A) applies, 28 days".

(3) After subsection (4) insert—

"(4A) This subsection applies where the person against whom the enforcement order would be made is a member of, or is represented by, a representative body, and that body operates a consumer code which has been approved by—

(a) an enforcer, other than a designated enforcer which is not a public body,

(b) a body which represents an enforcer mentioned in paragraph (a),

(c) a group of enforcers mentioned in paragraph (a), or

(d) a community interest company whose objects include the approval of consumer codes.

(4B) In subsection (4A)—

"consumer code" means a code of practice or other document (however described) intended, with a view to safeguarding or promoting the interests of consumers, to regulate by any means the conduct of persons engaged in the supply of goods or services to consumers (or the conduct of their employees or representatives), and

"representative body" means an organisation established to represent the interests of two or more businesses in a particular sector or area, and for this purpose "business" has the meaning it bears in section 210."

6 In section 217 (enforcement orders), after subsection (10) insert—

"(10A) An enforcement order may require a person against whom the order is made to take enhanced consumer measures (defined in section 219A) within a period specified by the court.

(10B) An undertaking under subsection (9) may include a further undertaking by the person to take enhanced consumer measures within a period specified in the undertaking.

(10C) Subsections (10A) and (10B) are subject to section 219C in a case where the application for the enforcement order was made by a designated enforcer which is not a public body.

(10D) Where a person is required by an enforcement order or an undertaking under this section to take enhanced consumer measures, the order or undertaking may include requirements as to the provision of information or documents to the court by the person in order that the court may determine if the person is taking those measures."

7 In section 219 (undertakings), after subsection (5) insert—

"(5ZA) An undertaking under this section may include a further undertaking by the person—

(a) to take enhanced consumer measures (defined in section 219A) within a period specified in the undertaking, and

(b) where such measures are included, to provide information or documents to the enforcer in order that the enforcer may determine if the person is taking those measures.

(5ZB) Subsection (5ZA) is subject to section 219C in a case where the enforcer is a designated enforcer which is not a public body."

8 After section 219 insert—

"219A Definition of enhanced consumer measures

"219A "219A Definition of enhanced consumer measures

(1) In this Part, enhanced consumer measures are measures (not excluded by subsection (5)) falling within—

(a) the redress category described in subsection (2),

(b) the compliance category described in subsection (3), or

(c) the choice category described in subsection (4).

(2) The measures in the redress category are—

(a) measures offering compensation or other redress to consumers who have suffered loss as a result of the conduct which has given rise to the enforcement order or undertaking,

(b) where the conduct referred to in paragraph (a) relates to a contract, measures offering such consumers the option to terminate (but not vary) that contract,

(c) where such consumers cannot be identified, or cannot be identified without disproportionate cost to the subject of the enforcement order or undertaking, measures intended to be in the collective interests of consumers.

(3) The measures in the compliance category are measures intended to prevent or reduce the risk of the occurrence or repetition of the conduct to which the enforcement order or undertaking relates (including measures with that purpose which may have the effect of improving compliance with consumer law more generally).

(4) The measures in the choice category are measures intended to enable consumers to choose more effectively between persons supplying or seeking to supply goods or services.

(5) The following are not enhanced consumer measures—

(a) a publication requirement included in an enforcement order as described in section 217(8),

(b) a publication requirement included in an undertaking accepted by the court as described in section 217(10), or

(c) a publication requirement included in an undertaking accepted by a CPC enforcer as described in section 219(5A)(a).

219B Inclusion of enhanced consumer measures etc.

219B 219B Inclusion of enhanced consumer measures etc.

(1) An enforcement order or undertaking may include only such enhanced consumer measures as the court or enforcer (as the case may be) considers to be just and reasonable.

(2) For the purposes of subsection (1) the court or enforcer must in particular consider whether any proposed enhanced consumer measures are proportionate, taking into account—

(a) the likely benefit of the measures to consumers,

(b) the costs likely to be incurred by the subject of the enforcement order or undertaking, and

(c) the likely cost to consumers of obtaining the benefit of the measures.

(3) The costs referred to in subsection (2)(b) are—

(a) the cost of the measures, and

(b) the reasonable administrative costs associated with taking the measures.

(4) An enforcement order or undertaking may include enhanced consumer measures in the redress category—

(a) only in a loss case, and

(b) only if the court or enforcer (as the case may be) is satisfied that the cost of such measures to the subject of the enforcement order or undertaking is unlikely to be more than the sum of the losses suffered by consumers as a result of the conduct which has given rise to the enforcement order or undertaking.

(5) The cost referred to in subsection (4)(b) does not include the administrative costs associated with taking the measures.

(6) Subsection (7) applies if an enforcement order or undertaking includes enhanced consumer measures offering compensation and a settlement agreement is entered into in connection with the payment of compensation.

(7) A waiver of a person's rights in the settlement agreement is not valid if it is a waiver of the right to bring civil proceedings in respect of conduct other than the conduct which has given rise to the enforcement order or undertaking.

(8) The following definitions apply for the purposes of subsection (4)(a).

(9) In the case of an enforcement order or undertaking under section 217, "a loss case" means a case in which—

(a) subsection (1) of that section applies (a finding that a person has engaged in conduct which constitutes an infringement), and

(b) consumers have suffered loss as a result of that conduct.

(10) In the case of an undertaking under section 219, "a loss case" means a case in which—

(a) subsection (3)(a) or (b) of that section applies (a belief that a person has engaged or is engaging in conduct which constitutes an infringement), and

(b) consumers have suffered loss as a result of that conduct.

219C Availability of enhanced consumer measures to private enforcers

219C 219C Availability of enhanced consumer measures to private enforcers

(1) An enforcement order made on the application of a designated enforcer which is not a public body may require a person to take enhanced consumer measures only if the following conditions are satisfied.

(2) An undertaking given under section 217(9) following an application for an enforcement order made by a designated enforcer which is not a public body, or an undertaking given to such an enforcer under section 219, may include a further undertaking by a person to take enhanced consumer measures only if the following conditions are satisfied.

(3) The first condition is that the enforcer is specified for the purposes of this section by order made by the Secretary of State.

(4) The second condition is that the enhanced consumer measures do not directly benefit the enforcer or an associated undertaking.

(5) Enhanced consumer measures which directly benefit an enforcer or an associated undertaking include, in particular, measures which—

(a) require a person to pay money to the enforcer or associated undertaking,

(b) require a person to participate in a scheme which is designed to recommend persons supplying or seeking to supply goods or services to consumers and which is administered by the the enforcer or associated undertaking, or

(c) would give the enforcer or associated undertaking a commercial advantage over any of its competitors.

(6) The Secretary of State may make an order under subsection (3) specifying an enforcer only if the Secretary of State is satisfied that to do so is likely to—

(a) improve the availability to consumers of redress for infringements to which the enforcer's designation relates,

(b) improve the availability to consumers of information which enables them to choose more effectively between persons supplying or seeking to supply goods or services, or

(c) improve compliance with consumer law.

(7) The Secretary of State may make an order under subsection (3) specifying an enforcer only if the functions of the enforcer under this Part have been specified under section 24 of the Legislative and Regulatory Reform Act 2006 (functions to which principles under section 21 and code of practice under section 22 apply), to the extent that they are capable of being so specified.

(8) The power to make an order under subsection (3)—

(a) is exercisable by statutory instrument subject to annulment in pursuance of a resolution of either House of Parliament;

(b) includes power to make incidental, supplementary, consequential, transitional, transitory or saving provision.

(9) Subsection (10) applies if—

(a) an enforcer exercises a function in relation to a person by virtue of subsection (1) or (2),

(b) that function is a relevant function for the purposes of Part 2 (co-ordination of regulatory enforcement) of the Regulatory Enforcement and Sanctions Act 2008, and

(c) a primary authority (within the meaning of that Part) has given advice or guidance under section 27(1) of that Act—

(i) to that person in relation to that function, or

(ii) to other local authorities (within the meaning of that Part) with that function as to how they should exercise it in relation to that person.

(10) The enforcer must, in exercising the function in relation to that person, act consistently with that advice or guidance.

(11) In this section "associated undertaking", in relation to a designated enforcer, means—

(a) a parent undertaking or subsidiary undertaking of the enforcer, or

(b) a subsidiary undertaking of a parent undertaking of the enforcer,

and for this purpose "parent undertaking" and "subsidiary undertaking" have the meanings given by section 1162 of the Companies Act 2006."

9 (1) Section 220 (further proceedings) is amended as follows.

(2) After subsection (1) insert—

"(1A) This section does not apply in the case of a failure to comply with an order or undertaking which consists only of a failure to provide information or documents required by the order or undertaking as described in section 217(10D)."

(3) In subsection (2), for "In such a case the CMA" substitute "Any CPC enforcer".

(4) In subsection (5)—

(a) in the opening words, for "sections 215 and 217 or 218 (as the case may be)" substitute "sections 215, 217 or 218 (as the case may be) and 219A, 219B and 219C",

(b) for paragraph (c) substitute—

"(c) section 217(9), (10), (10B) and (11) must be ignored, and section 217(10C) and (10D) must be ignored to the extent that they relate to an undertaking under section 217(9);",

(c) after paragraph (d) insert—

"(e) sections 219A, 219B and 219C must be ignored to the extent that they relate to an undertaking under section 217(9) or 219."

10 In section 229 (advice and information), after subsection (1) insert—

"(1A) As soon as is reasonably practicable after the commencement of Schedule 5 to the Consumer Rights Act 2015 (investigatory powers etc.) the CMA must prepare and publish advice and information with a view to—

(a) explaining the provisions of that Schedule, so far as they relate to investigatory powers exercised for the purposes set out in paragraphs 13(2) and (3) and 19 of that Schedule, to persons who are likely to be affected by them, and

(b) indicating how the CMA expects such provisions to operate."

SCHEDULE 8

Section 81

PRIVATE ACTIONS IN COMPETITION LAW

PART 1

COMPETITION ACT 1998

1 The Competition Act 1998 is amended in accordance with this Part.

2 For the heading of Chapter 4 of Part 1, substitute "Appeals, proceedings before the Tribunal and settlements relating to infringements of competition law".

3 For the cross-heading preceding section 46, substitute "Appeals and proceedings before the Tribunal".

4 (1) For section 47A substitute—

"47A Proceedings before the Tribunal: claims for damages etc.

"47A "47A Proceedings before the Tribunal: claims for damages etc.

(1) A person may make a claim to which this section applies in proceedings before the Tribunal, subject to the provisions of this Act and Tribunal rules.

(2) This section applies to a claim of a kind specified in subsection (3) which a person who has suffered loss or damage may make in civil proceedings brought in any part of the United Kingdom in respect of an infringement decision or an alleged infringement of—

(a) the Chapter I prohibition,
(b) the Chapter II prohibition,
(c) the prohibition in Article 101(1), or
(d) the prohibition in Article 102.

(3) The claims are—

(a) a claim for damages;
(b) any other claim for a sum of money;
(c) in proceedings in England and Wales or Northern Ireland, a claim for an injunction.

(4) For the purpose of identifying claims which may be made in civil proceedings, any limitation rules or rules relating to prescription that would apply in such proceedings are to be disregarded.

(5) The right to make a claim in proceedings under this section does not affect the right to bring any other proceedings in respect of the claim.

(6) In this Part (except in section 49C) "infringement decision" means—

(a) a decision of the CMA that the Chapter I prohibition, the Chapter II prohibition, the prohibition in Article 101(1) or the prohibition in Article 102 has been infringed,
(b) a decision of the Tribunal on an appeal from a decision of the CMA that the Chapter I prohibition, the Chapter II prohibition, the

prohibition in Article 101(1) or the prohibition in Article 102 has been infringed, or

(c) a decision of the Commission that the prohibition in Article 101(1) or the prohibition in Article 102 has been infringed."

(2) Section 47A of the Competition Act 1998 (as substituted by sub-paragraph (1)) applies to claims arising before the commencement of this paragraph as it applies to claims arising after that time.

5 (1) For section 47B substitute—

"47B Collective proceedings before the Tribunal

"47B "47B Collective proceedings before the Tribunal

(1) Subject to the provisions of this Act and Tribunal rules, proceedings may be brought before the Tribunal combining two or more claims to which section 47A applies ("collective proceedings").

(2) Collective proceedings must be commenced by a person who proposes to be the representative in those proceedings.

(3) The following points apply in relation to claims in collective proceedings—

(a) it is not a requirement that all of the claims should be against all of the defendants to the proceedings,

(b) the proceedings may combine claims which have been made in proceedings under section 47A and claims which have not, and

(c) a claim which has been made in proceedings under section 47A may be continued in collective proceedings only with the consent of the person who made that claim.

(4) Collective proceedings may be continued only if the Tribunal makes a collective proceedings order.

(5) The Tribunal may make a collective proceedings order only—

(a) if it considers that the person who brought the proceedings is a person who, if the order were made, the Tribunal could authorise to act as the representative in those proceedings in accordance with subsection (8), and

(b) in respect of claims which are eligible for inclusion in collective proceedings.

(6) Claims are eligible for inclusion in collective proceedings only if the Tribunal considers that they raise the same, similar or related issues of fact or law and are suitable to be brought in collective proceedings.

(7) A collective proceedings order must include the following matters—

(a) authorisation of the person who brought the proceedings to act as the representative in those proceedings,

(b) description of a class of persons whose claims are eligible for inclusion in the proceedings, and

(c) specification of the proceedings as opt-in collective proceedings or opt-out collective proceedings (see subsections (10) and (11)).

(8) The Tribunal may authorise a person to act as the representative in collective proceedings—

(a) whether or not that person is a person falling within the class of persons described in the collective proceedings order for those proceedings (a "class member"), but

(b) only if the Tribunal considers that it is just and reasonable for that person to act as a representative in those proceedings.

(9) The Tribunal may vary or revoke a collective proceedings order at any time.

(10) "Opt-in collective proceedings" are collective proceedings which are brought on behalf of each class member who opts in by notifying the representative, in a manner and by a time specified, that the claim should be included in the collective proceedings.

(11) "Opt-out collective proceedings" are collective proceedings which are brought on behalf of each class member except—

(a) any class member who opts out by notifying the representative, in a manner and by a time specified, that the claim should not be included in the collective proceedings, and

(b) any class member who—

(i) is not domiciled in the United Kingdom at a time specified, and

(ii) does not, in a manner and by a time specified, opt in by notifying the representative that the claim should be included in the collective proceedings.

(12) Where the Tribunal gives a judgment or makes an order in collective proceedings, the judgment or order is binding on all represented persons, except as otherwise specified.

(13) The right to make a claim in collective proceedings does not affect the right to bring any other proceedings in respect of the claim.

(14) In this section and in section 47C, "specified" means specified in a direction made by the Tribunal."

(2) Section 47B of the Competition Act 1998 (as substituted by sub-paragraph (1)) applies to claims arising before the commencement of this paragraph as it applies to claims arising after that time.

6 After section 47B (as substituted by paragraph 5) insert—

"47C Collective proceedings: damages and costs

"47C "47C Collective proceedings: damages and costs

(1) The Tribunal may not award exemplary damages in collective proceedings.

(2) The Tribunal may make an award of damages in collective proceedings without undertaking an assessment of the amount of damages recoverable in respect of the claim of each represented person.

(3) Where the Tribunal makes an award of damages in opt-out collective proceedings, the Tribunal must make an order providing for the damages to be paid on behalf of the represented persons to—

(a) the representative, or

(b) such person other than a represented person as the Tribunal thinks fit.

(4) Where the Tribunal makes an award of damages in opt-in collective proceedings, the Tribunal may make an order as described in subsection (3).

(5) Subject to subsection (6), where the Tribunal makes an award of damages in opt-out collective proceedings, any damages not claimed by the represented persons within a specified period must be paid to the charity for the time being prescribed by order made by the Lord Chancellor under section 194(8) of the Legal Services Act 2007.

(6) In a case within subsection (5) the Tribunal may order that all or part of any damages not claimed by the represented persons within a specified period is instead to be paid to the representative in respect of all or part of the costs or expenses incurred by the representative in connection with the proceedings.

(7) The Secretary of State may by order amend subsection (5) so as to substitute a different charity for the one for the time being specified in that subsection.

(8) A damages-based agreement is unenforceable if it relates to opt-out collective proceedings.

(9) In this section—

(a) "charity" means a body, or the trustees of a trust, established for charitable purposes only;

(b) "damages" (except in the term "exemplary damages") includes any sum of money which may be awarded by the Tribunal in collective proceedings (other than costs or expenses);

(c) "damages-based agreement" has the meaning given in section 58AA(3) of the Courts and Legal Services Act 1990."

7 After section 47C (inserted by paragraph 6) insert—

"47D Proceedings under section 47A or collective proceedings: injunctions etc.

"47D "47D Proceedings under section 47A or collective proceedings: injunctions etc.

(1) An injunction granted by the Tribunal in proceedings under section 47A or in collective proceedings—

(a) has the same effect as an injunction granted by the High Court, and

(b) is enforceable as if it were an injunction granted by the High Court.

(2) In deciding whether to grant an injunction in proceedings under section 47A or in collective proceedings, the Tribunal must—

(a) in proceedings in England and Wales, apply the principles which the High Court would apply in deciding whether to grant an injunction under section 37(1) of the Senior Courts Act 1981, and

(b) in proceedings in Northern Ireland, apply the principles that the High Court would apply in deciding whether to grant an injunction.

(3) Subsection (2) is subject to Tribunal rules which make provision of the kind mentioned in paragraph 15A(3) of Schedule 4 to the Enterprise Act 2002 (undertakings as to damages in relation to claims subject to the fast-track procedure)."

8 (1) After section 47D (inserted by paragraph 7) insert—

"47E Limitation or prescriptive periods for proceedings under section 47A and collective proceedings

"47E "47E Limitation or prescriptive periods for proceedings under section 47A and collective proceedings

(1) Subsection (2) applies in respect of a claim to which section 47A applies, for the purposes of determining the limitation or prescriptive period which would apply in respect of the claim if it were to be made in—

(a) proceedings under section 47A, or

(b) collective proceedings at the commencement of those proceedings.

(2) Where this subsection applies—

(a) in the case of proceedings in England and Wales, the Limitation Act 1980 applies as if the claim were an action in a court of law;

(b) in the case of proceedings in Scotland, the Prescription and Limitation (Scotland) Act 1973 applies as if the claim related to an obligation to which section 6 of that Act applies;

(c) in the case of proceedings in Northern Ireland, the Limitation (Northern Ireland) Order 1989 applies as if the claim were an action in a court established by law.

(3) Where a claim is made in collective proceedings at the commencement of those proceedings ("the section 47B claim"), subsections (4) to (6) apply for the purpose of determining the limitation or prescriptive period which would apply in respect of the claim if it were subsequently to be made in proceedings under section 47A.

(4) The running of the limitation or prescriptive period in respect of the claim is suspended from the date on which the collective proceedings are commenced.

(5) Following suspension under subsection (4), the running of the limitation or prescriptive period in respect of the claim resumes on the date on which any of the following occurs—

(a) the Tribunal declines to make a collective proceedings order in respect of the collective proceedings;

(b) the Tribunal makes a collective proceedings order in respect of the collective proceedings, but the order does not provide that the section 47B claim is eligible for inclusion in the proceedings;

(c) the Tribunal rejects the section 47B claim;

(d) in the case of opt-in collective proceedings, the period within which a person may choose to have the section 47B claim included in the proceedings expires without the person having done so;

(e) in the case of opt-out collective proceedings—
(i) a person domiciled in the United Kingdom chooses (within the period in which such a choice may be made) to have the section 47B claim excluded from the collective proceedings, or
(ii) the period within which a person not domiciled in the United Kingdom may choose to have the section 47B claim included in the collective proceedings expires without the person having done so;
(f) the section 47B claim is withdrawn;
(g) the Tribunal revokes the collective proceedings order in respect of the collective proceedings;
(h) the Tribunal varies the collective proceedings order in such a way that the section 47B claim is no longer included in the collective proceedings;
(i) the section 47B claim is settled with or without the Tribunal's approval;
(j) the section 47B claim is dismissed, discontinued or otherwise disposed of without an adjudication on the merits.

(6) Where the running of the limitation or prescriptive period in respect of the claim resumes under subsection (5) but the period would otherwise expire before the end of the period of six months beginning with the date of that resumption, the period is treated as expiring at the end of that six month period.

(7) This section has effect subject to any provision in Tribunal rules which defers the date on which the limitation or prescriptive period begins in relation to claims in proceedings under section 47A or in collective proceedings."

(2) Section 47E of the Competition Act 1998 does not apply in relation to claims arising before the commencement of this paragraph.

9 (1) Section 49 (further appeals) is amended in accordance with this paragraph.

(2) In subsection (1)—
(a) at the end of paragraph (a) insert "and", and
(b) omit paragraph (b) and the "and" at the end of that paragraph.

(3) After subsection (1) insert—

"(1A) An appeal lies to the appropriate court on a point of law arising from a decision of the Tribunal in proceedings under section 47A or in collective proceedings—
(a) as to the award of damages or other sum (other than a decision on costs or expenses), or
(b) as to the grant of an injunction.

(1B) An appeal lies to the appropriate court from a decision of the Tribunal in proceedings under section 47A or in collective proceedings as to the amount of an award of damages or other sum (other than the amount of costs or expenses).

(1C) An appeal under subsection (1A) arising from a decision in respect of a stand-alone claim may include consideration of a point of law arising from a finding of the Tribunal as to an infringement of a prohibition listed in section 47A(2).

(1D) In subsection (1C) "a stand-alone claim" is a claim—

(a) in respect of an alleged infringement of a prohibition listed in section 47A(2), and

(b) made in proceedings under section 47A or included in collective proceedings."

(4) In subsection (2)(a), at the beginning insert "except as provided by subsection (2A),".

(5) After subsection (2) insert—

"(2A) An appeal from a decision of the Tribunal in respect of a claim included in collective proceedings may be brought only by the representative in those proceedings or by a defendant to that claim."

10 (1) After section 49 insert—

"Settlements relating to infringements of competition law

49A Collective settlements: where a collective proceedings order has been made

49A 49A Collective settlements: where a collective proceedings order has been made

(1) The Tribunal may, in accordance with this section and Tribunal rules, make an order approving the settlement of claims in collective proceedings (a "collective settlement") where—

(a) a collective proceedings order has been made in respect of the claims, and

(b) the Tribunal has specified that the proceedings are opt-out collective proceedings.

(2) An application for approval of a proposed collective settlement must be made to the Tribunal by the representative and the defendant in the collective proceedings.

(3) The representative and the defendant must provide agreed details of the claims to be settled by the proposed collective settlement and the proposed terms of that settlement.

(4) Where there is more than one defendant in the collective proceedings, "defendant" in subsections (2) and (3) means such of the defendants as wish to be bound by the proposed collective settlement.

(5) The Tribunal may make an order approving a proposed collective settlement only if satisfied that its terms are just and reasonable.

(6) On the date on which the Tribunal approves a collective settlement—

(a) if the period within which persons may opt out of or (in the case of persons not domiciled in the United Kingdom) opt in to the collective proceedings has expired, subsections (8) and (10) apply so as to determine the persons bound by the settlement;

(b) if that period has not yet expired, subsections (9) and (10) apply so as to determine the persons bound by the settlement.

(7) If the period within which persons may opt out of the collective proceedings expires on a different date from the period within which persons not domiciled in the United Kingdom may opt in to the collective proceedings, the references in subsection (6) to the expiry of a period are to the expiry of whichever of those periods expires later.

(8) Where this subsection applies, a collective settlement approved by the Tribunal is binding on all persons falling within the class of persons described in the collective proceedings order who—

(a) were domiciled in the United Kingdom at the time specified for the purposes of determining domicile in relation to the collective proceedings (see section 47B(11)(b)(i)) and did not opt out of those proceedings, or

(b) opted in to the collective proceedings.

(9) Where this subsection applies, a collective settlement approved by the Tribunal is binding on all persons falling within the class of persons described in the collective proceedings order.

(10) But a collective settlement is not binding on a person who—

(a) opts out by notifying the representative, in a manner and by a time specified, that the claim should not be included in the collective settlement, or

(b) is not domiciled in the United Kingdom at a time specified, and does not, in a manner and by a time specified, opt in by notifying the representative that the claim should be included in the collective settlement.

(11) This section does not affect a person's right to offer to settle opt-in collective proceedings.

(12) In this section and in section 49B, "specified" means specified in a direction made by the Tribunal."

(2) Section 49A of the Competition Act 1998 applies to claims arising before the commencement of this paragraph as it applies to claims arising after that time.

11 (1) After section 49A (inserted by paragraph 10) insert—

"49B Collective settlements: where a collective proceedings order has not been made

"49B "49B Collective settlements: where a collective proceedings order has not been made

(1) The Tribunal may, in accordance with this section and Tribunal rules, make an order approving the settlement of claims (a "collective settlement") where—

(a) a collective proceedings order has not been made in respect of the claims, but

(b) if collective proceedings were brought, the claims could be made at the commencement of the proceedings (disregarding any limitation or prescriptive period applicable to a claim in collective proceedings).

(2) An application for approval of a proposed collective settlement must be made to the Tribunal by—

(a) a person who proposes to be the settlement representative in relation to the collective settlement, and

(b) the person who, if collective proceedings were brought in respect of the claims, would be a defendant in those proceedings (or, where more than one person would be a defendant in those proceedings, such of those persons as wish to be bound by the proposed collective settlement).

(3) The persons applying to the Tribunal under subsection (2) must provide agreed details of the claims to be settled by the proposed collective settlement and the proposed terms of that settlement.

(4) The Tribunal may make an order approving a proposed collective settlement (see subsection (8)) only if it first makes a collective settlement order.

(5) The Tribunal may make a collective settlement order only—

(a) if it considers that the person described in subsection (2)(a) is a person who, if the order were made, the Tribunal could authorise to act as the settlement representative in relation to the collective settlement in accordance with subsection (7), and

(b) in respect of claims which, if collective proceedings were brought, would be eligible for inclusion in the proceedings (see section 47B(6)).

(6) A collective settlement order must include the following matters—

(a) authorisation of the person described in subsection (2)(a) to act as the settlement representative in relation to the collective settlement, and

(b) description of a class of persons whose claims fall within subsection (5)(b).

(7) The Tribunal may authorise a person to act as the settlement representative in relation to a collective settlement—

(a) whether or not that person is a person falling within the class of persons described in the collective settlement order for that settlement, but

(b) only if the Tribunal considers that it is just and reasonable for that person to act as the settlement representative in relation to that settlement.

(8) Where the Tribunal has made a collective settlement order, it may make an order approving a proposed collective settlement only if satisfied that its terms are just and reasonable.

(9) A collective settlement approved by the Tribunal is binding on all persons falling within the class of persons described in the collective settlement order.

(10) But a collective settlement is not binding on a person who—

(a) opts out by notifying the settlement representative, in a manner and by a time specified, that the claim should not be included in the collective settlement, or

(b) is not domiciled in the United Kingdom at a time specified, and does not, in a manner and by a time specified, opt in by notifying the settlement representative that the claim should be included in the collective settlement.

(11) In this section, "settlement representative" means a person who is authorised by a collective settlement order to act in relation to a collective settlement."

(2) Section 49B of the Competition Act 1998 applies to claims arising before the commencement of this paragraph as it applies to claims arising after that time.

12 After section 49B (inserted by paragraph 11) insert—

"49C Approval of redress schemes by the CMA

"49C "49C Approval of redress schemes by the CMA

(1) A person may apply to the CMA for approval of a redress scheme.

(2) The CMA may consider an application before the infringement decision to which the redress scheme relates has been made, but may approve the scheme only—

(a) after that decision has been made, or

(b) in the case of a decision of the CMA, at the same time as that decision is made.

(3) In deciding whether to approve a redress scheme, the CMA may take into account the amount or value of compensation offered under the scheme.

(4) The CMA may approve a redress scheme under subsection (2)(b) subject to a condition or conditions requiring the provision of further information about the operation of the scheme (including about the amount or value of compensation to be offered under the scheme or how this will be determined).

(5) If the CMA approves a redress scheme subject to such a condition, it may—

(a) approve the scheme subject to other conditions;

(b) withdraw approval from the scheme if any conditions imposed under subsection (4) or paragraph (a) are not met;

(c) approve a redress scheme as a replacement for the original scheme (but may not approve that scheme subject to conditions).

(6) An approved scheme may not be varied by the CMA or the compensating party.

(7) But, where the CMA approves a redress scheme subject to a condition of the kind mentioned in subsection (4), subsection (6) does not prevent further information provided in accordance with the condition from forming part of the terms of the scheme.

(8) The Secretary of State may make regulations relating to the approval of redress schemes, and the regulations may in particular—

(a) make provision as to the procedure governing an application for approval of a redress scheme, including the information to be provided with the application;

(b) provide that the CMA may approve a redress scheme only if it has been devised according to a process specified in the regulations;

(c) provide that the CMA may approve a redress scheme only if it is in a form, or contains terms, specified in the regulations (which may include terms requiring a settlement agreement under the scheme to be in a form, or contain terms, specified in the regulations);

(d) provide that the CMA may approve a redress scheme only if (so far as the CMA can judge from facts known to it) the scheme is intended to be administered in a manner specified in the regulations;

(e) describe factors which the CMA may or must take into account, or may not take into account, in deciding whether to approve a redress scheme.

(9) The CMA must publish guidance with regard to—

(a) applications for approval of redress schemes,

(b) the approval of redress schemes, and

(c) the enforcement of approved schemes, and in particular as to the criteria which the CMA intends to adopt in deciding whether to bring proceedings under section 49E(4).

(10) Guidance under subsection (9) must be approved by the Secretary of State before it is published.

(11) In this section and sections 49D and 49E—

"approved scheme" means a redress scheme approved by the CMA,

"compensating party" means a person offering compensation under an approved scheme,

"infringement decision" means—

(a) a decision of the CMA that the Chapter I prohibition, the Chapter II prohibition, the prohibition in Article 101(1) or the prohibition in Article 102 has been infringed, or

(b) a decision of the Commission that the prohibition in Article 101(1) or the prohibition in Article 102 has been infringed, and

"redress scheme" means a scheme under which a person offers compensation in consequence of an infringement decision made in respect of that person.

(12) For the purposes of this section and section 49E, "compensation"—

(a) may be monetary or non-monetary, and

(b) may be offered to persons who have not suffered a loss as a result of the infringement decision to which the redress scheme relates.

49D Redress schemes: recovery of costs

49D 49D Redress schemes: recovery of costs

(1) The CMA may require a person making an application for approval of a redress scheme to pay some or all of the CMA's reasonable costs relating to the application.

(2) A requirement to pay costs is imposed by giving that person written notice specifying—

- (a) the amount to be paid,
- (b) how that amount has been calculated, and
- (c) by when that amount must be paid.

(3) A person required to pay costs under this section may appeal to the Tribunal against the amount.

(4) Where costs required to be paid under this section relate to an approved scheme, the CMA may withdraw approval from that scheme if the costs have not been paid by the date specified in accordance with subsection (2)(c).

(5) Costs required to be paid under this section are recoverable by the CMA as a debt.

49E Enforcement of approved schemes

49E 49E Enforcement of approved schemes

(1) A compensating party is under a duty to comply with the terms of an approved scheme ("the duty").

(2) The duty is owed to any person entitled to compensation under the terms of the approved scheme.

(3) Where such a person suffers loss or damage as a result of a breach of the duty, the person may bring civil proceedings before the court for damages, an injunction or interdict or any other appropriate relief or remedy.

(4) Where the CMA considers that the compensating party is in breach of the duty, the CMA may bring civil proceedings before the court for an injunction or interdict or any other appropriate relief or remedy.

(5) Subsection (4) is without prejudice to any right that a person has to bring proceedings under subsection (3).

(6) In any proceedings brought under subsection (3) or (4), it is a defence for the compensating party to show that it took all reasonable steps to comply with the duty.

(7) Where the CMA considers that it is no longer appropriate for the compensating party to be subject to the duty, the CMA may give notice in writing to that party stating that it is released from the duty.

(8) Where a person has entered into a settlement agreement with the compensating party, that agreement remains enforceable notwithstanding the release of the compensating party under subsection (7) from the duty.

(9) In this section "the court" means—
(a) in England and Wales, the High Court or the county court,
(b) in Northern Ireland, the High Court or a county court,
(c) in Scotland, the Court of Session or the sheriff."

13 (1) Section 58 (findings of fact by CMA) is amended in accordance with this paragraph.

(2) In subsection (1), after "the court" insert "or the Tribunal".

(3) In subsection (2)—
(a) in the definition of "Part I proceedings", before paragraph (a) insert—
"(za) in respect of an infringement decision;", and
(b) in the definition of "relevant party", in paragraphs (a) and (b), for "is alleged to have infringed the prohibition" substitute "has been found to have infringed the prohibition or is alleged to have infringed the prohibition (as the case may be)".

(4) In subsection (3)—
(a) after "Rules of court" insert "or Tribunal rules", and
(b) after "the court" insert "or the Tribunal".

(5) After subsection (3) insert—

"(4) In this section "the court" means—
(a) in England and Wales or Northern Ireland, the High Court,
(b) in Scotland, the Court of Session or the sheriff."

14 (1) For section 58A substitute—

"58A Infringement decisions

"58A "58A Infringement decisions

(1) This section applies to a claim in respect of an infringement decision which is brought in proceedings—
(a) before the court, or
(b) before the Tribunal under section 47A or 47B.

(2) The court or the Tribunal is bound by the infringement decision once it has become final.

(3) An infringement decision specified in section 47A(6)(a) or (b) becomes final—
(a) when the time for appealing against that decision expires without an appeal having been brought;
(b) where the decision is specified in section 47A(6)(a) and an appeal has been brought against the decision under section 46 or 47, when that appeal—
(i) has been withdrawn, dismissed or otherwise discontinued, or
(ii) has confirmed the infringement decision and the time for making any further appeal against that confirmatory

decision expires without a further appeal having been brought;

(c) where an appeal has been brought in relation to the decision under section 49, when that appeal—

(i) in the case of an appeal against the infringement decision or against a decision which confirmed the infringement decision, has been withdrawn, dismissed or otherwise discontinued, or

(ii) has confirmed the infringement decision and the time for making any further appeal to the Supreme Court against that confirmatory decision expires without a further appeal having been brought; or

(d) where an appeal has been brought to the Supreme Court in relation to the decision, when that appeal—

(i) in the case of an appeal against a decision which confirmed the infringement decision, has been withdrawn, dismissed or otherwise discontinued, or

(ii) has confirmed the infringement decision.

(4) An infringement decision specified in section 47A(6)(c) becomes final—

(a) when the time for appealing against that decision in the European Court expires without an appeal having been brought; or

(b) where such an appeal has been brought against the decision, when that appeal—

(i) has been withdrawn, dismissed or otherwise discontinued, or

(ii) has confirmed the infringement decision.

(5) This section applies to the extent that the court or the Tribunal would not otherwise be bound by the infringement decision in question.

(6) In this section "the court" means—

(a) in England and Wales or Northern Ireland, the High Court,

(b) in Scotland, the Court of Session or the sheriff."

(2) Section 58A of the Competition Act 1998 (as substituted by sub-paragraph (1)) does not apply in relation to decisions made before the commencement of this paragraph.

15 (1) Section 59 (interpretation of Part 1) is amended in accordance with this paragraph.

(2) In subsection (1), at the appropriate places insert—

"“class member” has the meaning given in section 47B(8)(a);";

"“collective proceedings” has the meaning given in section 47B(1);";

"“collective proceedings order” means an order made by the Tribunal authorising the continuance of collective proceedings;";

"“infringement decision”, except in section 49C, has the meaning given in section 47A(6);";

"“injunction” includes an interim injunction;";

"“opt-in collective proceedings” has the meaning given in section 47B(10);";

"“opt-out collective proceedings” has the meaning given in section 47B(11);"

"""representative" means a person who is authorised by a collective proceedings order to bring collective proceedings;";

"""represented person" means a class member who—

(a) has opted in to opt-in collective proceedings,

(b) was domiciled in the United Kingdom at the time specified for the purposes of determining domicile (see section 47B(11)(b)(i)) and has not opted out of opt-out collective proceedings, or

(c) has opted in to opt-out collective proceedings;".

(3) In subsection (1), in the definition of "the court", before "58" insert "49E,".

(4) After subsection (1) insert—

"(1A) In this Part, in respect of proceedings in Scotland, "defendant" is to be read as "defender".

(1B) Sections 41, 42, 45 and 46 of the Civil Jurisdiction and Judgments Act 1982 apply for the purpose of determining whether a person is regarded as "domiciled in the United Kingdom" for the purposes of this Part."

16 In section 71 (regulations, orders and rules), after subsection (4)(ca) insert—

"(cb) section 47C(7),".

17 (1) Schedule 8 (appeals) is amended in accordance with this paragraph.

(2) In paragraph 2(1), for "46 or 47" substitute "46, 47 or 49D(3)".

(3) After paragraph 3A insert—

"3B (1) This paragraph applies to an appeal under section 49D(3).

(2) The Tribunal must determine the appeal on the merits by reference to the grounds of appeal set out in the notice of appeal.

(3) The Tribunal may—

(a) approve the amount of costs which is the subject of the appeal, or

(b) impose a requirement to pay costs of a different amount.

(4) The Tribunal may also give such directions, or take such other steps, as the CMA could itself have given or taken.

(5) A requirement imposed by the Tribunal under sub-paragraph (3)(b) has the same effect, and may be enforced in the same manner, as a requirement imposed by the CMA under section 49D."

PART 2

ENTERPRISE ACT 2002

18 The Enterprise Act 2002 is amended in accordance with this Part.

19 (1) Section 14 (constitution of Tribunal for particular proceedings and its decisions) is amended as follows.

(2) In subsection (1), after "before it" insert ", including proceedings relating to the approval of a collective settlement under section 49A or 49B of the 1998 Act,".

(3) After subsection (1) insert—

"(1A) But in the case of proceedings relating to a claim under section 47A of the 1998 Act which is subject to the fast-track procedure (as described in Tribunal rules), the Tribunal may consist of a chairman only."

20 In section 15 (Tribunal rules), in subsection (1), at the end insert ", including proceedings relating to the approval of a collective settlement under section 49A or 49B of the 1998 Act."

21 In section 16 (transfers of certain proceedings to and from Tribunal), in subsection (5), for "High Court or the Court of Session of" substitute "court of all or any part of".

22 Schedule 4 (Tribunal: procedure) is amended in accordance with the following paragraphs of this Part.

23 In paragraph 1 (decisions of the Tribunal), for sub-paragraph (1)(a) substitute—

"(a) state the reasons for the decision;

(aa) state whether the decision was unanimous or taken by a majority or, where proceedings are heard by a chairman only, state that fact;".

24 After paragraph 1 insert—

"1A Enforcement of injunctions in England and Wales and Northern Ireland

1A (1) Where a person ("A") fails to comply with an injunction granted by the Tribunal in proceedings under section 47A or 47B of the 1998 Act, the Tribunal may certify the matter to the High Court.

(2) The High Court may enquire into the matter.

(3) If, after hearing any witnesses who may be produced against or on behalf of A, and any statement made by or on behalf of A, the High Court is satisfied that A would have been in contempt of court if the injunction had been granted by the High Court, the High Court may deal with A as if A were in contempt."

25 In each of paragraphs 4(c) and 5(1)(c)—

(a) for "47B(6)" substitute "47C(3) or (4)"; and

(b) for "specified body concerned" substitute "representative in the proceedings under section 47B of that Act".

26 In paragraph 6—

(a) for sub-paragraph (a) substitute—

"(a) awards damages to a person in respect of a claim made or continued on behalf of that person (but is not the subject of an order under section 47C(3) or (4) of that Act); or";

(b) in sub-paragraph (b)—

(i) for "an individual" substitute "a person",

(ii) for "his behalf" substitute "behalf of that person"; and

(c) in the full-out words at the end, for "individual" substitute "person".

27 In paragraph 7—

(a) for "specified body" substitute "representative"; and

(b) for "individual" substitute "person".

28 In paragraph 9—

(a) the existing provision is numbered as sub-paragraph (1), and

(b) after that provision insert—

"(2) In this Schedule, where a paragraph is capable of applying to proceedings relating to the approval of a collective settlement under section 49A or 49B of the 1998 Act, any reference in that paragraph to "proceedings" includes a reference to those proceedings."

29 In paragraph 11(2), for paragraph (a) substitute—

"(a) make further provision as to procedural aspects of the operation of the limitation or prescriptive periods in relation to claims which may be made in proceedings under section 47A of the 1998 Act, as set out in section 47E(3) to (6) of that Act;".

30 For paragraph 13 substitute—

"13 (1) Tribunal rules may provide for the Tribunal—

(a) to reject a claim made under section 47A of the 1998 Act or a section 47B claim if it considers that there are no reasonable grounds for making it;

(b) to reject a section 47B claim if—

(i) the Tribunal declines to make a collective proceedings order in respect of the proceedings under section 47B of the 1998 Act,

(ii) the Tribunal makes a collective proceedings order in respect of the proceedings, but the order does not provide that the claim in question is eligible for inclusion in the proceedings,

(iii) the Tribunal revokes the collective proceedings order in respect of the proceedings, or

(iv) the Tribunal varies the collective proceedings order in such a way that the claim in question is no longer included in the proceedings;

(c) to reject a section 47B claim if the claim had been previously made in proceedings under section 47A of the 1998 Act by a person who has not consented to its being continued in proceedings under section 47B of that Act.

(2) In this paragraph, "a section 47B claim" means a claim made in proceedings under section 47B of the 1998 Act at the commencement of those proceedings."

31 After paragraph 15 insert—

"15A Fast-track procedure

15A (1) Tribunal rules may make provision in relation to a fast-track procedure for claims made in proceedings under section 47A of the 1998 Act, including describing the factors relevant to determining whether a claim is suitable to be dealt with according to that procedure.

(2) Tribunal rules may make different provision for claims in proceedings under section 47A of the 1998 Act which are and which are not subject to the fast-track procedure.

(3) Tribunal rules may, in particular, provide for the Tribunal to—

(a) grant an interim injunction on a claim in proceedings under section 47A of the 1998 Act which is subject to the fast-track procedure to a person who has not given an undertaking as to damages, or

(b) impose a cap on the amount that a person may be required to pay under an undertaking as to damages given on the granting of such an interim injunction.

(4) In sub-paragraph (3) "an undertaking as to damages" means an undertaking to pay damages which a person sustains as a result of the interim injunction and which the Tribunal considers the person to whom the injunction is granted should pay.

15B Collective proceedings

15B (1) Tribunal rules may make provision in relation to collective proceedings under section 47B of the 1998 Act.

(2) Rules under sub-paragraph (1) must in particular make provision as to the following matters—

(a) the procedure governing an application for a collective proceedings order;

(b) the factors which the Tribunal must take into account in deciding whether a claim is suitable to be brought in collective proceedings (but rules need not make provision in connection with the determination as to whether claims raise the same, similar or related issues of fact or law);

(c) the factors which the Tribunal must take into account in deciding whether to authorise a person to act as a representative in collective proceedings;

(d) the procedure by which the Tribunal is to reach a decision as to whether to make a collective proceedings order;

(e) the procedure by which a person may opt in or opt out of collective proceedings;

(f) the factors which the Tribunal must take into account in deciding whether to vary or revoke a collective proceedings order;

(g) the assessment of damages in collective proceedings;

(h) the payment of damages in collective proceedings, including the procedure for publicising an award of damages;

(i) the effect of judgments and orders in collective proceedings.

15C Collective settlements

15C (1) Tribunal rules may make provision in relation to collective settlements under sections 49A and 49B of the 1998 Act.

(2) Rules under sub-paragraph (1) must in particular make provision as to the following matters—

(a) the procedure governing an application for approval of a proposed collective settlement;

(b) where section 49B applies, the factors which the Tribunal must take into account in deciding whether to make a collective settlement order (but rules need not make provision in connection with the determination as to whether claims raise the same, similar or related issues of fact or law);

(c) where section 49B applies, the factors which the Tribunal must take into account in deciding whether to authorise a person to act as a settlement representative in relation to a collective settlement;

(d) where section 49B applies, the procedure by which the Tribunal is to reach a decision as to whether to make a collective settlement order;

(e) the factors which the Tribunal must take into account in deciding whether to approve a proposed collective settlement;

(f) the procedure by which the Tribunal is to reach a decision as to whether to approve a collective settlement;

(g) the procedure by which a person may opt in or opt out of a collective settlement;

(h) the payment of compensation under a collective settlement, including the procedure for publicising a compensation award."

32 In paragraph 17 (conduct of the hearing)—

(a) after sub-paragraph (1)(h) insert—

"(ha) allowing the Tribunal to order payments in respect of the representation of a party to proceedings under section 47A or 47B of the 1998 Act, where the representation by a legal representative was provided free of charge;";

(b) in sub-paragraph (2)—

(i) for "an individual" substitute "a person"; and

(ii) for "that individual" substitute "that person";

(c) after sub-paragraph (2) insert—

"(2A) Rules under sub-paragraph (1)(h) may provide for costs or expenses to be awarded to or against a person on whose behalf a claim is made or continued in proceedings under section 47B of the 1998 Act in respect of an application in the proceedings made by that person (where that application is not made by the representative in the proceedings on that person's behalf)."; and

(d) in sub-paragraph (3), for "an individual" substitute "a person".

33 After paragraph 20 insert—

"20A Stay or sist of proceedings

20A (1) In relation to proceedings in England and Wales or Northern Ireland under section 47A or 47B of the 1998 Act, Tribunal rules may make provision as to the stay of the proceedings, including as to—

(a) the circumstances in which a stay may be ordered or removed at the request of a party to the proceedings,

(b) the circumstances in which the proceedings may be stayed at the instance of the Tribunal, and

(c) the procedure to be followed.

(2) In relation to proceedings in Scotland under section 47A or 47B of the 1998 Act, Tribunal rules may make provision as to the sist of the proceedings, including as to—

(a) the circumstances in which a sist may be granted or recalled at the request of a party to the proceedings,

(b) the circumstances in which the proceedings may be sisted at the instance of the Tribunal, and

(c) the procedure to be followed.

(3) Rules under sub-paragraph (1) or (2) may in particular make provision in relation to the stay or sist of proceedings under section 47A or 47B which relate to a claim in respect of an infringement decision (as defined in section 47A(6)) which has not become final (see section 58A of the 1998 Act)."

34 After paragraph 21 insert—

"21A Injunctions

21A Tribunal rules may make provision in relation to the grant of injunctions (including interim injunctions) in proceedings under section 47A or 47B of the 1998 Act."

35 In paragraph 23(3), for "an individual" substitute "a person".

36 In paragraph 25, after "transfer of" insert "all or any part of".

PART 3

COURTS AND LEGAL SERVICES ACT 1990

37 In the Courts and Legal Services Act 1990, in section 58AA (damages-based agreements), after subsection (10) insert—

"(11) Subsection (1) is subject to section 47C(8) of the Competition Act 1998."

SCHEDULE 9

Section 87

DUTY OF LETTING AGENTS TO PUBLICISE FEES: FINANCIAL PENALTIES

Notice of intent

1 (1) Before imposing a financial penalty on a letting agent for a breach of a duty imposed by or under section 83, a local weights and measures authority must serve a notice on the agent of its proposal to do so (a "notice of intent").

(2) The notice of intent must be served before the end of the period of 6 months beginning with the first day on which the authority has sufficient evidence of the agent's breach, subject to sub-paragraph (3).

(3) If the agent is in breach of the duty on that day, and the breach continues beyond the end of that day, the notice of intent may be served—

(a) at any time when the breach is continuing, or

(b) within the period of 6 months beginning with the last day on which the breach occurs.

(4) The notice of intent must set out—

(a) the amount of the proposed financial penalty,

(b) the reasons for proposing to impose the penalty, and

(c) information about the right to make representations under paragraph 2.

Right to make representations

2 The letting agent may, within the period of 28 days beginning with the day after that on which the notice of intent was sent, make written representations to the local weights and measures authority about the proposal to impose a financial penalty on the agent.

Final notice

3 (1) After the end of the period mentioned in paragraph 2 the local weights and measures authority must—

(a) decide whether to impose a financial penalty on the letting agent, and

(b) if it decides to do so, decide the amount of the penalty.

(2) If the authority decides to impose a financial penalty on the agent, it must serve a notice on the agent (a "final notice") imposing that penalty.

(3) The final notice must require the penalty to be paid within the period of 28 days beginning with the day after that on which the notice was sent.

(4) The final notice must set out—

(a) the amount of the financial penalty,

(b) the reasons for imposing the penalty,

(c) information about how to pay the penalty,

(d) the period for payment of the penalty,

(e) information about rights of appeal, and

(f) the consequences of failure to comply with the notice.

Withdrawal or amendment of notice

4 (1) A local weights and measures authority may at any time—

(a) withdraw a notice of intent or final notice, or

(b) reduce the amount specified in a notice of intent or final notice.

(2) The power in sub-paragraph (1) is to be exercised by giving notice in writing to the letting agent on whom the notice was served.

Appeals

5 (1) A letting agent on whom a final notice is served may appeal against that notice to—

(a) the First-tier Tribunal, in the case of a notice served by a local weights and measures authority in England, or

(b) the residential property tribunal, in the case of a notice served by a local weights and measures authority in Wales.

(2) The grounds for an appeal under this paragraph are that—

(a) the decision to impose a financial penalty was based on an error of fact,

(b) the decision was wrong in law,

(c) the amount of the financial penalty is unreasonable, or

(d) the decision was unreasonable for any other reason.

(3) An appeal under this paragraph to the residential property tribunal must be brought within the period of 28 days beginning with the day after that on which the final notice was sent.

(4) If a letting agent appeals under this paragraph, the final notice is suspended until the appeal is finally determined or withdrawn.

(5) On an appeal under this paragraph the First-tier Tribunal or (as the case may be) the residential property tribunal may quash, confirm or vary the final notice.

(6) The final notice may not be varied under sub-paragraph (5) so as to make it impose a financial penalty of more than £5,000.

Recovery of financial penalty

6 (1) This paragraph applies if a letting agent does not pay the whole or any part of a financial penalty which, in accordance with this Schedule, the agent is liable to pay.

(2) The local weights and measures authority which imposed the financial penalty may recover the penalty or part on the order of the county court as if it were payable under an order of that court.

(3) In proceedings before the county court for the recovery of a financial penalty or part of a financial penalty, a certificate which is—

(a) signed by the chief finance officer of the local weights and measures authority which imposed the penalty, and

(b) states that the amount due has not been received by a date specified in the certificate,

is conclusive evidence of that fact.

(4) A certificate to that effect and purporting to be so signed is to be treated as being so signed unless the contrary is proved.

(5) A local weights and measures authority may use the proceeds of a financial penalty for the purposes of any of its functions (whether or not the function is expressed to be a function of a local weights and measures authority).

(6) In this paragraph "chief finance officer" has the same meaning as in section 5 of the Local Government and Housing Act 1989.

SCHEDULE 10

Section 93

SECONDARY TICKETING: FINANCIAL PENALTIES

Notice of intent

1 (1) Before imposing a financial penalty on a person for a breach of a duty or prohibition imposed by Chapter 5 of Part 3, an enforcement authority must serve a notice on the person of its proposal to do so (a "notice of intent").

(2) The notice of intent must be served before the end of the period of 6 months beginning with the first day on which the authority has sufficient evidence of the person's breach, subject to sub-paragraph (3).

(3) If the person is in breach of the duty or prohibition on that day, and the breach continues beyond the end of that day, the notice of intent may be served—

(a) at any time when the breach is continuing, or

(b) within the period of 6 months beginning with the last day on which the breach occurs.

(4) The notice of intent must set out—

(a) the amount of the proposed financial penalty,

(b) the reasons for proposing to impose the penalty, and

(c) information about the right to make representations under paragraph 2.

Right to make representations

2 A person on whom a notice of intent is served may, within the period of 28 days beginning with the day after that on which the notice was sent, make written representations to the enforcement authority about the proposal to impose a financial penalty on the person.

Final notice

3 (1) After the end of the period mentioned in paragraph 2 the enforcement authority must—

(a) decide whether to impose a financial penalty on the person, and

(b) if it decides to do so, decide the amount of the penalty.

(2) If the authority decides to impose a financial penalty on the person, it must serve a notice on the person (a "final notice") imposing that penalty.

(3) The final notice must require the penalty to be paid within the period of 28 days beginning with the day after that on which the notice was sent.

(4) The final notice must set out—

(a) the amount of the financial penalty,

(b) the reasons for imposing the penalty,

(c) information about how to pay the penalty,

(d) the period for payment of the penalty,

(e) information about rights of appeal, and

(f) the consequences of failure to comply with the notice.

Withdrawal or amendment of notice

4 (1) The enforcement authority may at any time—

(a) withdraw a notice of intent or final notice, or

(b) reduce the amount specified in a notice of intent or final notice.

(2) The power in sub-paragraph (1) is to be exercised by giving notice in writing to the person on whom the notice was served.

Appeals

5 (1) A person on whom a final notice is served may appeal against that notice—

(a) in England and Wales and Scotland, to the First-tier Tribunal;

(b) in Northern Ireland, to a county court.

(2) The grounds for an appeal under this paragraph are that—

(a) the decision to impose a financial penalty was based on an error of fact,

(b) the decision was wrong in law,

(c) the amount of the financial penalty is unreasonable, or

(d) the decision was unreasonable for any other reason.

(3) If a person appeals under this paragraph, the final notice is suspended until the appeal is finally determined or withdrawn.

(4) On an appeal under this paragraph the First-tier Tribunal or the court may quash, confirm or vary the final notice.

(5) The final notice may not be varied under sub-paragraph (4) so as to make it impose a financial penalty of more than £5,000.

Recovery of financial penalty

6 (1) This paragraph applies if a person does not pay the whole or any part of a financial penalty which, in accordance with this Schedule, the person is liable to pay.

(2) In England and Wales the local weights and measures authority which imposed the financial penalty may recover the penalty or part on the order of the county court as if it were payable under an order of that court.

(3) In Scotland the penalty may be enforced in the same manner as an extract registered decree arbitral bearing a warrant for execution issued by the sheriff court of any sheriffdom in Scotland.

(4) In Northern Ireland the Department of Enterprise, Trade and Investment may recover the penalty or part on the order of a county court as if it were payable under an order of that court.

(5) In proceedings before the court for the recovery of a financial penalty or part of a financial penalty, a certificate which is—

(a) signed by the chief finance officer of the local weights and measures authority which imposed the penalty or (as the case may be) issued by the Department of Enterprise, Trade and Investment, and

(b) states that the amount due has not been received by a date specified in the certificate, is conclusive evidence of that fact.

(6) A certificate to that effect and purporting to be so signed or issued is to be treated as being so signed or issued unless the contrary is proved.

(7) A local weights and measures authority may use the proceeds of a financial penalty for the purposes of any of its functions (whether or not the function is expressed to be a function of a local weights and measures authority).

(8) In this paragraph "chief finance officer" has the same meaning as in section 5 of the Local Government and Housing Act 1989.

Adapted and published by GRANGIS under the OGL Licence 3.0.

www.nationalarchives.gov.uk/doc/open-government-licence/version/3/

GRANGIS - UK PUBLISHING 2022.

Thank you for taking the time to leave us a review regarding this version

★★★★★

For further inquiries, contact us at:
www.grangis.com / contact@grangis.com

www.ingramcontent.com/pod-product-compliance
Lightning Source LLC
LaVergne TN
LVHW060212210926
848481LV00008B/2711
* 9 7 9 8 8 8 5 5 9 0 1 3 6 *